A MEDLEY OF
POETRY

Esther Adams

A Medley Of Poetry

Copyright © 2021 by Esther Adams.

Paperback ISBN: 978-1-952982-58-3
Hardcover ISBN: 978-1-63812-190-9
Ebook ISBN: 978-1-952982-59-0

All rights reserved. No part in this book may be produced and transmitted in any form or by any means, electronic, or mechanical, including photocopying, recording, or by any information storage and retrieval system, without permission in writing from the copyright owner.

The views expressed in this work are solely those of the author and do not necessarily reflect the views of the publisher hereby disclaims any responsibility for them.

Published by Pen Culture Solutions 01/21/2022

Pen Culture Solutions
1-888-727-7204 (USA)
1-800-950-458 (Australia)
support@penculturesolutions.com

Contents

A Big House 1
A Morning Prayer 3
A Mother's Guilt 5
A New Baby 7
A New Earth 8
A Parent's Regret 10
A Prayer For Strength 14
A Prayer Of Gratitude 16
A Prayer Of Thanks 18
A Psych Nurse's Grudge 20
A Wish For A Newborn 22
About Me 23
Accept Me 25
America 26
Annette 28
Be Thankful 30
Bib And Diaper 32
Black And White 33
Boy George 35
Broken Toys 37
Buddha 38

Creation	40
Don't Cry For Me	42
Don't Grumble	44
Eleni	46
Empty Me	48
Equality	50
Eulogy For Matthew	52
Euthanasia	53
For Matthew 1	55
Frances	56
Gay	57
Good Doers	59
Greed	61
Grey Day	63
Happy Birthday Miranda	65
Happy Birthday Timothy	66
He Loves Us All	67
Her Ladyship	69
Humanity	71
I Am Safe	72
I Am Free	73
I Changed	74
I Would Like	77
Is It You?	79
Jailed	81
Jemima	82
Kids In A Playground	83
Lawrence	87
Legalise Them	89

Life	92
Little Girl	94
Little Things	95
Matthew	96
Mr. Trump	98
My Daughter	101
My Mobile	103
My Mother-In-Law	105
My Prayer for Elliot	107
My Sister	109
My Sister Carole	111
Myrtle Tree	112
Newborn	113
Norman	115
Ode To A Tree	116
Old Age	117
Old Lady	119
Pearls Of Wisdom	120
Poverty	121
Precious Things	123
Pride	125
Psych Hospital	127
Racism	129
Red	131
Resurrection	133
Revenge	136
Shame	138
Sobering	140
Speak Not	142

Spring	144
The Beggar	146
The Cross	149
The Same Way Lord	151
The Servant Nurse	163
The Tooth Fairy	165
Timothy	166
Tired	168
To Jemima	170
To The Groom	171
Transgender	173
Tribute To Joyce Costa	175
Tribute To Matthew	176
Understand	177
Victoria	179
We Failed You	181
We Let You Go	185
What Are You?	187
Zdenka	190

I dedicate this book to my daughter Miranda, and my sons Timothy and Daniel, my grandchildren Jemima, Victoria ,Elliot, Lawrence and their families.

> with all my love.
>
> Yiayia

29 August 2020

A Big House

We build big houses we can't afford to keep
We want large spaces we think we will need

We say that extra bedroom will come handy
That family room is important most certainly

We don't know it, but most times we won't use it
They will keep the teen-agers away, good isn't it?

Banging music we don't hear, mess we don't see
We have peace of mind; we think it's a blessing, is it?

When a few years later, we look back we cry bitterly
Kids have grown up, spent their day upstairs comfortably.

They were in the huge house somewhere, being busy
 What were they doing? now I wish with them I could be

I will sing the praises of the old three-bedroom house
Cheap to heat and cool, your kids were always around

I'd hear what they said, I'd know what they were about
I sing the praises of a well-designed three-bedroom house

To all of you, young people a huge house you don't need
Unless you want to show off, build one to meet your need.

I was looking at my three-bedroom, old design house and thought to myself, I'd like a bit more room in the dining room. I compared it with bigger, roomier houses I lived in, and yeas later I realised that the children had spent a lot of time on their own upstairs, I saw very little of them, before I knew it, they were independent, and I felt that I missed out in their growing up hears. I felt sad. This poem was born out of sadness.

16 August 2020

A Morning Prayer

Lord, let me kneel before You at the start of my day
Just for a while and bring my needs to You say
Please, take care of us, keep us safe for another day

The sun is rising the stars are fading in the vast sky
We need Your strength to toil just for another day
Please send Your angels to protect us for just for today.

I want others to see that You are within me today
I want to tell them that the load You give us isn't heavy
I want to say You will hold our hand You'll lead the way

I want to shout loudly; I want to sing and to everybody say
His love endures for ever, He will be with you again today
Don't worry, trust Him, put your hand in His He'll lead the way

Lord I ask that you cleanse me and with me remain
Give me the strength to do the right thing for today
And go to my bed in peace and sleep the night away.

Esther

Feb 4 2019

A Mother's Guilt

As we grow older, we become 'soft in the brain', and much softer in the heart
I wish someone had told me, there' is a better way to bring your children up
You don't need to belt them, so that good they'll be when they will grow up.

Then again, I might have said, they are my children, don't interfere, I know best
I get a lump in my throat, tears run down my face, thinking of what I have done.
The cane isn't used now, but do parents know what to do when children play up?

The painting of the crying child, I can't bear to see, wondering who painted it
Perhaps it was his father or his mother, many years later prompted by guilt.
Another chance were I given, knowing now what I do, a better parent I'd be.

I loved them dearly, but bringing up children I didn't know how, no idea I had.
I feel so very sad when I look back, I tell myself 'it's too late now, try to forget.
It doesn't make it easier to bear, sadly one chance only with each child we get.

My daughter's cries I still hear, her tears I still see, I smacked her very hard that day
My high heel shoes she wore: 'Mummy' crying she said 'a lady like you, I want to be'
Forgive me my darling girl, a good mother I tried to be but as usual I failed miserably.

Esther

I was painting in Melton today and as usual my mind was racing again. I thought of when Miranda was nearly four years old. She took my high heel shoes and wore them playing in the cubby house. Coming outside she fell. Hearing her cries, I ran to see what was wrong. Seeing her wearing my shoes I thought she did the wrong thing. I picked her up and instead of comforting her I smacked her. She cried then, I am crying now. Oh, that I had then, the wisdom I have now!

14 Feb 2020

A New Baby

A precious little girl came into your life
May she grow to be mature and wise
May she bring you loads of joy and pride
May she live a long and productive life.

For a boy

A precious little boy came into your life
May he grow to be mature and wise
May he bring you loads of joy and pride
May he live a long and productive life.

Esther

8/9/2015
Euston UK

A New Earth

Oh, how I wish I could be an innocent child once again
To forget racism, war, homelessness, hunger and pain
To walk by my fellow man without fear and say 'hale'

To know that God filled this world with different things
Creatures of all kinds, small plants, grass and tall trees
And ordered them to live together in harmony and peace

He intended that we should all care for earth and fields
So that flowers, vegies and trees could bear heavy yields
And that nobody would need to say 'give us food please'

Last He created Adam 'n Eve complete with all their bits
And I am sure he gave them both, all kinds of genes
To fill this earth with beautiful and colourful beings

But greed took over and created rich and many poor
Big companies cared for their own gains not for all
Told mothers 'the milk in our tins is good for a newborn'.

How I wish I could see the earth made brand new
With food and houses for all, not just for a lucky few
A world in unity and peace where there are no poor.

A world where people take care of grass and tall tree
Where children play without fear and are happy 'n free
And where races will live together in peace and harmony

Can we do it? Yes, if we all join hands in this.

And for sure, when 'the stone that was cut without hands fills the earth' (The Bible, book of Daniel)

Esther

A Parent's Regret

A baby boy was born to my family just twenty years ago
He was healthy and chubby 'he's so handsome' said we all
That he was jolly, gentle and sensitive, was easy to see
Elliot was his name, but 'Buddha' his nickname came to be.

He laughed and he giggled and played with his puppy a lot
He walked and he talked clearly, much earlier than most.
He played with other kids, but happy alone was he too,
He played with toys and read books by the time he was two.

He was bigger and smarter than his siblings, his kin and his peers
Much more was expected of him; to his parents he was very dear
When he was told 'you're a big boy now, you can do better than this'
His head he would hang in shame, but in his eyes, were no tears.

He grew up to be gentle, unselfish and generous to a fault
To him money was not made flat to be stacked, but round to roll
And when in his pocket he'd spent it before he got to the store.
He helped anyone he could; loved to sleep but loved people more.

Little brother got him in trouble, big sister could do no wrong
Often, he was blamed for things he was not responsible for.
He never stood up for himself, he carried the blame alone
He was treated unfairly for a long time, this for sure I know.

He carried the pain of unfairness deep in his young soul
Never ever, a word of complaint to anyone he uttered at all.
Like venom, the injustice poisoned and wrecked his tender soul
'Yiayia, I know drugs fuck my brain, but they help me forget it all'.

Lord, I can't argue with that, but please help him to understand
That parents too were young once, they learned as they went along.
We try so hard a good job to do, but on our faces, flat we all fall.
We pat ourselves on the back, we are conceited, but till we reflect

We praise ourselves, but we cry when we think it through.
The job we thought we did so well, wasn't so good after all.
We wish we could change it, but only one chance we get that's all
Old heads on young shoulders won't sit, try it, you'll fail, that I bet.

Ourselves we hate, through torture and pain all our lives we go
But alas! The damage we have caused them we can never undo
We can only go to them humbly and sincerely say 'so sorry son,
I know we've hurt you a lot, but ourselves we've hurt even more'

I feel so guilty, a coward I was, I didn't defend him I didn't stand up
I had no courage; I had no guts to say to his mother 'it wasn't his fault'.
Forgive me my loving grandson, in your magnanimous soul
I know, I am sure, that you will find it easy to forgive us all.

Elliot, please forgive us, this will help our troubled souls to still
Please try to forget all the injustices, this your soul too, will heal
We love you, respect you, to us a wonderful son you'll always be

We respect your choices no matter what,
we will love you still.

Your ever loving Yiayia

I wrote this poem having visited my son and his family in Wagga Wagga. My two grandchildren Victoria and Elliot and their cousin were in the swimming pool. The two girls were making a terrible racket throwing water on each other and shrieking, yelling and fooling about like teenage girls do. Elliot standing at the edge of pool, his arms behind his back, watching them with a smile on his face, and so was I. Frances who was inside and unaware of what was going on, raced outside and without asking what was going on, she ordered 16-year-old Elliot out of the pool and sent him to his room. He obediently did, without explaining what happened. I was stunned! When I recovered, I went to his room where he was reading and told him how sorry I was, it was not fair and that he got the wrong end of the stick. He looked up at me with those big brown eyes of his full of sadness; he uttered two words only: 'As usual'. That upset me even more. The expression of hurt in his eyes was exactly the same as in Miranda's eyes when she was eight years old. I went home and wrote this poem. I cried and castigated myself for not explaining to Frances what had happened. I am sure she would have understood I will always blame myself for not defending him. This poem also applies to Miranda and countless other kids. I hope they find it in their hearts to forgive us as Miranda did.

Esther

4/07/13

A Prayer For Strength

Lord, let me pause before I start my day
Just for a moment and humbly to You say
Thank You Lord for the light of a new day
Thank You for hope, courage, and for faith.
Thank You for pleasures and for the pain.

Thank You for giving me the choice to be and do
And showing me the way that I should go
Thank You again for accepting me as I am
'Bruises and ulcers, sores, warts' and all.
Thank You for holding my hand and leading me on.

Lord, give me the faith to believe and clearly see
That nothing escapes Your eye, You know everything,
The little sparrow falling to the ground You always see.
'Worthless it is' to others we say, but not so to Thee
And I know that the pain of my soul, You also see.

Please give me the strength to stand just for today
And let me bring to You my fears, and my pain

And with a grateful heart before Your feet to lay.
Filled with courage, give me leave to go and say
Thank You, my Lord, for the light of another day.

When my heart is aching and my faith is shaking, I always find solace, comfort and strength in God.

Having written this, my mind is at peace my worry has gone and a load has been lifted off my heart. Even though I know of the danger Elliot is in, and that ultimately it is his decision which way he wants to go. It is not in the nature of God to take away from us the freedom of choice He has given us in the first place. All I ask is that God will show him the way and let him choose what he will. May he choose wisely is my prayer for him.

Esther

27 May 2013

A Prayer Of Gratitude

Thank You Lord for hearing me when I pray
Thank you for taking my fears and troubles away
Thank You for the 'peace that passes all understanding'
Thank You for holding me up when my knees give way.

Thank You Lord for reassuring me when I am afraid
Thank You for not forsaking me when I miserably fail.
Thank You for rushing to my help and softly to me say,
'Child, hush' your cries I hear, I'm never too far away.

Thank You Lord, for in Your word plainly to us You say
'Come, let us reason together I Am always the Same,
Loving, your needs I know, I'm willing and able to save
If you remember My promises, you'll never suffer pain'.

Lord I know Your arm is not too weak all of us to save
This in many places in Your word, plainly to us You say
'Surely the arm of the Lord is not too weak to save'
Just come to me, your troubles before My feet to lay.

Comfort is ours just for the asking, I feel unburdened and free knowing that God loves our children more than we ourselves do 'if you being evil want to give your children good things how much more your father who is in heaven', Jesus said. I find this very comforting.

I woke up this morning, went to the kitchen and looking at Elliot's photo a peace came over me, a peace which I have known many times before. All the fearful thoughts went away, hope and optimism filled my soul, I bowed my head and once again I thanked God, and wrote this prayer in just over 30 minutes

Esther

5/7/13

A Prayer Of Thanks

Lord let me kneel before You at the end of my day
Just for a while and with a thankful heart to humbly say
Thank You my God, for being with us for another day.
Thank You for watching over us and keeping us all safe.
Thank You for the strength you've given me to face our day.

The sun has set, the stars are shining bright in the night sky
My strength has ebbed, I am tired, my eyes are closing tight
Please send your holy angels to watch over us again tonight
In sweet dreams on their wings to Your heavenly home to rise
And raise us up again to do our work and Your will till night.

I want to praise You with my voice and work till the day I die,
I want others to see that the load You have given us is light
And when yoked with You, You, carry most of the weight

When our knees buckle, in Your Arms You carry us all the way.
I now bow before You and with Your saints I will sing and say,

"Holy, Holy, Holy Lord, is You Name".

Esther

12 Jan 2019

A Psych Nurse's Grudge

Once upon a time, sick people were referred to as 'Patients'
They had no rights, doctors were gods, and nurses their angels.
Then they became 'clients'. Rights they were given, and rightly so
They could say 'yes' to treatment had they chosen, or say 'no'.

Now, they are 'consumers' as in a shop. They are right, never wrong.
They refuse treatment if they choose, doctors have no say, like it or no.
They kick doors, smash windows, spit on us, we have no rights at all.
Unlucky 'consumers' they had a rough childhood, they had 'no fair go'.

Makes my blood boil! it's all one way, we too need some attention
We all had a rough trot, where are our rights? do we matter at all?
We are low paid for what we do, we are very tired, suffer exhaustion
Maybe one day I'll change jobs, will be a strip dancer, I will earn more.

Of the hundreds of people over the long years I have met
only three I heard say, I had a happy childhood all was well
The rest of us had a hard time, but we didn't turn out bad.
I often think of grandma, 'It's in the blood' she always said.

One day science could well say, 'It's all in the genes, too bad.

Esther

I wrote this poem while at hand-over at work. A particular patient's bad behaviour was being handed-over. Someone, sympathetically said 'Well, he had a difficult childhood'. That excuse makes me mad. Most of us had a difficult childhood, and as far as I am concerned, this should not be used as an excuse for bad behaviour. I stopped taking notes of the hand-over, and instead I wrote the first two verses of this poem and later, during my dinner break I added the rest.

17/7/13

A Wish For A Newborn

May he/she grow white and old
May what he/she what touches turn into gold
May he/she bring joy and pride
To you and your family for the rest of your life

I wrote this little verse/wish 5 years ago for Maria's little girl. Maria is my colleague who eight and a half years ago rang me at 6am and told me there was a permanent position available if I wanted to apply for it and I have been grateful to her ever since.

14 June 2020

About Me

What am I like? Quick tempered, impatient, intolerant and belligerent
As blunt as an old battle axe, hit people on the head with brute reality.
You scared me to death they said laughingly when they got to know me.

I can't tolerate lazy people, liars and cheats they are very hard to take.
They'll sit on their bum watching you work, won't help, make no mistake.
I want to shake liars say 'stop strangling the truth your story doesn't stake'.

I prefer thieves, to liars and cheats, you can lock up, yourself can defend
But with liars you can never be sure, you do not know where you stand.
What about the cheats? They are in between, they are sly, sit on the fence.

I know I am judging them harshly; Lord forgive me, I cannot help myself.
That's the downside of me, I am remind you just in case you will forget.
And my dearest, please, please don't exaggerate in singing my praises

For perfect I was not. I know, I accept and
I acknowledge this
You know I would be turning in my gave if
you omitted to say it.
We all have shortcomings, we've all sinned,
the good book says it

Esther

16/9/2015
Chingford UK

Accept Me

I will happily and willingly tell you my name
But please don't ask me where I am from yet
I am not from Venus I too was born on Earth.

Wearing a tag separates us, sets a division amongst us
We are all Earthlings regardless our colour and faith.
When we know each other better, I'll tell you my tale.

Accept me now just for being another person
With my strengths, weaknesses faults and virtues
I have likes, dislikes and foibles just like all others.

Our origins are not of importance this you would know
Whether we are black, white, rich or poor doesn't matter
Let's respect all for being human, not for what we own.

Esther

31 May 2020

America

"America needs security, not anarchy" Mr Trump tweets
"America needs justice not racism" the big mob screams
Mr Trump, black people are angry, suffered, you know this.

People are dying without justice at the hands of your police
They mustn't judge and kill; they are there to keep the peace.
They kill before judging; they 're not the law they do as they wish.

Mr Trump, the police have it wrong, it is not their job to kill
Their duty is to search for the law breaker and hand him in
They should not kill; justice must be done and must be seen.

Families are mourning the loss of loved ones not knowing why
Parents go to their graves crying, why did my son have to die?"
Mr Trump, how would you feel if it's your son the one to die?

Remember, black people were taken to America by brute force.

They were enslaved. downtrodden, beaten and exploited then
A man must stand up for his rights sooner or later it makes sense

No country should expect to enjoy law and order,
Justice always, but always, will go before peace
You can't fight violence with violence you know this.

Esther

I was watching the news this morning when I saw Trump's tweet saying "America needs security not anarchy". Again, I became angry at yet another life lost at the hands of the police. As far as I am concerned the police are not there to serve out justice, their duty is to catch the law breakers and hand them over to the courts of justice, for judgment, punishment or otherwise.

They are the law keepers not the justice servers.

1 March 2021

Annette

You are very loving, kind, thoughtful and powerful
You always look outside yourself and are grateful
You look at other peoples' problems and are thankful

Even in your greatest loss you showed no bitterness
You look forward to the day when there will be no sadness
You look for the positive in pain, you thank God in fullness.

Your heart is breaking, your eyes are overflowing with tears
You look back at the joy 'n love he brought you over the years
Joel was your pride and joy; your pain fills my eyes with tears.

He is gone too young; won't see him in this world again
But he won't be away from us, by our side he will remain
His kindness and helpfulness in our hearts will for ever stay

His voice we will always hear, it won't assuage the pain
He lived his short life trying to help others in every way
This fact will not be erased, in our hearts it will remain.

You and your family have my deepest sympathy

Esther
Your adopted sister

April 28 2021

Be Thankful

1. Do you wake up with pains and aches? please don't grumble
Be thankful to God you woke up at all, be humble.

2. Others are on a wheel chair, in a nursing home or bed bound
Be thankful you can still get out of bed, hobbling the toilet you found.

3. You can enjoy the sunshine, smell the roses and pluck the daisies
Admire a tall tree, hear a little bird sing, to me, this is just so amazing

4. You can still clean and feed yourself, a few pains and aches don't count
When you are utterly and completely dependant then you can grumble.

5. You are around your children and grandchildren with your family
Look outside yourself, others are suffering too, don't think selfishly.

Felt tired and down today. Made me a cup of tea and sat outside in the sun. I grumbled about my fatigue, pains and aches. Then I looked outside myself. I thought of little Alice. Just seven years old and suffering constant pain. I berated myself made me shut up, asked myself 'why am I complaining?

I wrote this little poem in less than half an hour and dedicate it to Alice, she is such a wonderful, brave little girl. I pray as she grows older she will overcome all her pain.

Nov 20 2019

Bib And Diaper

They say we start life with a bib and a diaper
We are wrinkly, dribble have no teeth or hair
And it is true we end up with a bib and a diaper
Except that the latter is bigger and much smellier.

Your teeth are no longer fixed in mouth
They clack, fall on your lap or on the ground
But that's how it is when we are grave bound
Sorry, but there is nothing we can do about.

We start without memory and end up without one
We start without awareness and end up without one
Our mind gives up, we become a burden to every one
And if we live too long, we won't escape it my dear one.

I was feeling low in spirits when I wrote this

Esther

1 July 2020

Black And White

Beyoncé, I'd like to remind you that neither black nor white is a colour
Remember, white reflects all colour whereas black absorbs it altogether
We must be very careful not to praise one and oppress the other.

I know that black people suffered discrimination because of their colour.
They were ill-treated, downtrodden abused by white men like no other
Now we must be careful not to reverse the tables and oppress the other.

"Black is beautiful" intelligent and gifted and so is yellow, red and white
The song says 'Red and yellow, black and white all are precious in His sight'
I would say, not one is perfect, we failed, 'we are all wretched in His sight'

We must try to be fair and respect each other, regardless of status or colour
This is the important thing not our riches, intelligence position or our colour
Remember we will all die one day, leaving everything we have to another.

"Shrouds have no pockets" and if they did, you wouldn't know it down under
It is greed that created suffering, pain and slavery on this earth like no other
Let's respect, and love our neighbour as ourselves, let us "love one another".

And Beyoncé just a black and white world would be a duotone and very dull
Let's open our eyes to the beauty of every race, let us include every colour
We are all unique on earth, we all have something to offer regardless our colour.

Esther

I was watching channel 2 this morning, when they promoted Beyoncé's new album about black colour. An undefined fear overcame me. I thought 'what would happen if the tables were turned?' I hate to think. All the years of suffering, pain and oppression of the black people would be poured out on this earth without mercy. Revenge would reign supreme with all her fury, no telling where it would end. I wouldn't like to be alive to see it. I hope and pray Forgiveness with her healing power and Reason with her calming influence, will reign supreme on this planet. And an apology and restoration would go a long way to achieve this and to 'make America great again'

Tue 18 June 2019

Boy George

Boy George, in this world you are one in a million
I don't give a damn what others say, it is my opinion
You are eccentric in the loveliest sense of the word.
There aren't too many like you in the whole world.

The lights are dazzling but your face lights up the stage
I love the music but best of all I love to watch your face
When you smile your dimples brighten the whole place
And I love watching you dressed up standing on the stage

Watching you I forget my troubles, you are such a treasure
With you in the show, is entertaining, gives me pleasure
The music and singing are wonderful, and the hour flies by
But you I like to watch best, you are a very, very sweet boy.

And I would really love to give you a bearhug someday.

Your admirer

I wrote this poem especially for you because watching you gives me much pleasure

Grandma Esther

Broken Toys

Like children bring their broken toys
With tears for us to mend
I brought my broken dreams to God
Because He is my friend.

But then I, instead of leaving Him
In peace to work alone
I hung around and I tried to help
With ways that were my own.

A last I snatched them back 'n crying I said
Why are You so slow I don't understand.
My child, He said what could I do?
You didn't let go; you never gave me a chance.

Author unknown,
Edited by Esther

20/02/2014

Buddha

You came to this world with a happy look on your 'dial'
Elliot was your name, but only till your first smile
It was angelic, contagious, happy and so Buddha like.

Your gentleness and unselfishness knew no bounds
Even as a young child you always wanted to help others
You took them in your care; you met them on their ground.

To encourage, support and love them was always your joy
No one was beyond your reach, whether a girl or a boy
You cared, and when in need, they only had to call 'ahoy'

Ready to comfort, to help them and their spirits to lift
You had it in you; helping others for you was a cinch
You came to this world for a purpose; the peace to keep.

Intelligent and good looking, pride was not in your heart
I often wonder if Buddha didn't come with you from the past
His great work to continue, his unselfish spirit to broadcast.

I hope and I pray his path in some way you will follow
Buddha's work was great and enduring, not at all hollow

You have what it takes; go ahead, to us all you can show.

Dearest Elliot

Wishing you a great 21st birthday, and many happy returns of the day. You have a great future ahead of you and there isn't much you can't achieve; of that, I am sure. I love you and always will no matter how you choose to live your life.

Your ever loving yiayia xoxoxoxo

25 August 2018

Creation

'In the beginning, God created the Heavens and the earth'
Six thousand years ago someone said. 'No this is a joke I said'
When was the beginning? rocks and earth another story tell.

God is infinite, limiting the infinite doesn't fit, doesn't go
Look up at the night skies, billions of stars are declaring so
'Like sand on the shore are His days' how many? do you know?

His spirit walked on this earth, guided and the future foretold,
To many people He spoke in riddles and dreams, in times of old
Daniel foretold the future, read the scriptures, how did he know?

Read ancient history, Daniel the man of God said it all before
In amazing detail described this earth's history from head to toe
'Daniel, write, knowledge shall increase, men shall run to and fro'.

In fear and trembling, but also in faith and
joy, I look forward too,
When the Ancient of days to this earth will
be coming very soon
To take us home to the stars, till He makes
this earth brand new.

I wrote this poem while at daughter's place in Kalorama. I woke up at 2:30am as usual. My shoulder was very sore. I prayed for healing and strength to finish the job at hand. As always, true to His promise, 'ask and it shall be given you' the pain went away. I thanked and praised God for yet another miracle in my life. I sat up and wrote this poem in about an hour.

Monday, 5 July 2019

Don't Cry For Me

I lived my life on earth and enjoyed it to the fullest
Often, I fell made many mistakes but tried my best
Tasted joys and sorrows the same as everybody else.

I have been privileged and blessed above many others
I have seen my children and grandchildren grow up
They are healthy and adjusted I can't ask more than that.

All I ask now is to see the dream He gave me come true
I will be happy to leave you then, please don't cry for me
I will join the ones I loved, will sleep till you too join me

Till that beautiful day when the loud trumpet will sound
Calling us to get up from the dust, and the dark ground
To meet again 'n live on a new earth without a dark cloud.

Try to live your life loving and forgiving each other
Please don't hold grudges against one another
Remember, hating hurts you more than the other.

It is better to love than to hate. I did my best He did the rest.

Esther

28 April 2021

Don't Grumble

Do you wake up with pains and aches? don't grumble
Stop! be thankful to God, you woke up at all, be humble.

Others are in a nursing home in a wheel chair or bed bound
Be grateful, you got out of bed, to the toilet your way found.

You can feed and clean yourself, a few pains and aches don't count
You enjoy the sunshine, in your garden flowers and herbs abound.

You can smell a rose, pluck a daisy, hear the birds sing, the bees buzz
Walk on the green grass, talk to a neighbour, it's a privilege don't fuss.

You are around your children and grandchildren you are with your family
Look outside yourself, others are suffering too, don't be selfish be grateful

I felt tired and down today. Sat out in the sun with a cup of tea. I grumbled about my fatigue and pains and aches. Then I looked outside myself. I thought of little Alice, just seven years old, has suffered pain all her short little life. I berated myself, I asked 'why am I complaining? What do I have to complain about? I shut up and instead of complaining I became grateful for a long, and healthy life well lived.

Esther

22/10/17

Eleni

You came to this world and were given a hard lot
You worked hard; you did the best with what you got
You had 3 children; you had to work you couldn't stop.

You were generous and kind beyond all measure
To you, giving was not a duty it was a pleasure
'Give' you always said 'the feeling is a treasure'.

You loved the land your soul had always been in it
No cold, no heat nor wind could keep you out of it
The land was your life, and you were always in it.

You wanted to live and die on the land, and you'd do so
But infirmity took over, you had no choice, you had to go
They took the girl out of the land, but not the land out of you

I loved you and will sorely miss you till the day we meet again.
Your loving sister

Esther

12 May 20021

Empty Me

Lord I come to you asking that You empty me from all I think I know
Then I can learn anew.
Lord empty my mind and my soul from all I've learned at school to make
room in me for You.

Lord, empty my mind and my soul from my enemy, the 'Ego' which fills my
soul.
Sadly, making me proud, leaving no room in my heart and mind for You.

Lord, empty me from all my parents, society, school and religion taught me
For I want to be empty and unprejudiced so that I can be taught just by You.

I want to see in Your word the difference in the mundane, the history, the holy
and the sinful
But above all, I long to commune daily through the Spirit and draw strength
for the day from You.

Lord I know this will never be if my mind and soul are filled by self-importance
and pride

As there will be no room in my mind and
soul for You. Please help me be humble
just like Jesus,

I now come humbly and sincerely ask that
You cleanse my soul from all that's ugly
in Your sight and all that,
I come to You empty, please fill me with Your
Spirit, enlighten me, open my eyes that
I can see Your truth and love.

Cleanse and purify me, come in, and with
Your Spirit live in me. Please fill me up and
filled I will be.
I will be in Jesus and He in me, I will see
Your love and mercies, Your power
available to me will be.

I woke up early feeling alert and refreshed. I wanted to understand the difference in the holy books of the world, between the mundane and the spiritual. Reading 'Osho' 'Walk without feet fly without wings think without a mind' helped me understand that the biggest obstacle in our growth generally and spiritually, is our ego, our prejudices and our self-importance.

For a long time now, I have been praying for cleansing not realising what I was really asking for. I wrote this prayer in about half an hour.

Esther

March 30 2019

Equality

There is no such thing as equality on this earth or in heaven
Please don't gasp, I'll tell you why, before you count to seven.
Up there is a King, a Prince, gate keepers angels, and archangels.

The Book says, man was created a little lower than the angels.
I know where you'll find equality, but it's not above the clouds
It's in the coffin, lonely, cold and still, six feet under the ground

Where rich and poor sleep together in the dark, cold ground
Where we are all equal and where money does not count
Where we are eaten by worms, and are covered with ground

Esther

I was looking around the ward today observing the patients, and I realised how some of them were better off financially than others. I thought of the community at large and the world and was saddened to realise that there is no equality anywhere, not even in heaven. Yes, there is peace, joy and justice for all, but not equality. Equality is only found in arithmetic and in the grave. If it is found anywhere else, I'd like to know about it.

27 April 2001

Eulogy For Matthew

Tears may dry but hearts for ever will sigh
You will always but always be by my side
Not a day goes by that I don't think of you
Sleep till the morning when we meet again.

I went to bed on the 10th of January wondering what to put in the Newspaper in Matthew's memory. This eulogy came to me in a dream on the 11th of January 2001. I forgot about it till I read it while putting the diary of that year in a USB. I have edited the one in the dream which it said

> Tears may dry, but hearts still cry,
> not a day goes by that I don't think of you.'
> Sleep till the morning.

Esther

18 August 2018

Euthanasia

I want my family around me, good bye to all of them to say
To hug and to tell them, to a better world I am going today
To say how much I love them, they have brightened my day
To admit my mistakes, all my failures bare before them to lay.

I don't want to be laying in a hospital bed languishing in pain
Too feeble to clean or feed myself, that will bring me shame.
I ask the government 'why do you want to have the last say?
After all it's my life, it should be my privilege, to choose day'.

I had no say in my coming to this world, I want a say when I go away
To choose the clothes and the place where for a little while I will lay
It is a wonderful feeling, knowing I had a choice, I did it all my way
To celebrate my life with song and dance, it will be a wonderful day.

I lived a long and productive life, did things my way, I had control
Now I am old, infirm, tired of life, lost interest, I really want to go
Who said you have the right to ignore my wishes and take control?
No Holy book ever said that suicide is a sin, only the Pope says so.

I want to die my way, listen to me, even if the Pope says 'no'
Religion has no right to dictate how I should or should not go
Let me make up my own mind, I will sort it out with my God.
If He decides I have sinned, He, not you, has the right to say so.

Esther

I was watching the news in bed this morning. The discussion was on people choosing their own governments. I thought of other choices people should be given. The current topic of euthanasia came to my mind. I put pen to paper and wrote this poem in about half an hour.

19 January 1999

For Matthew 1

My soul is in darkness and mourning deep
Because the loveliest and kindest of all
Passed away so suddenly, just last week

I heard this short poem in my dream when Matthew died suddenly 19 years ago. I still get upset when I think of him.

2 September 2020

Frances

What can I say about my dear Frances?
She is as bright and colourful as a rainbow
You want to know something? she'll know

If she doesn't know it, she'll work I out
Today or tomorrow, she'll find a solution
When she is resting her head on a cushion

Sharp witted, good with numbers and money
She can be as strong as steel or sweet as honey
Has a quick tongue, means no harm in any way.

She runs her household like an army barracks
Not a cushion out of place, not a book on a chair
Her drawers are tidy, you find things in blinkers.

Makes me feel inadequate, I can't even find my nickers

I was thinking of my dear daughter-in-law today. I thought of her strengths and weaknesses. I concluded she has many more positives than negatives, she is intelligent has drive and is more tolerant and tidier than I'll ever be. Love her.

20 Feb 2020

Gay

He is well built, handsome and intelligent 'but he is gay
He is competent, holds a responsible job 'but he is gay'
Talked to his mother who in sadness said, 'but he is gay'

Is this a fault? Have you ever thought that 'he was born gay?
Do you blame him for his looks? Why blame him 'for being gay?
He can't help the genes he inherited; he was 'conceived gay'.

He is a law-abiding citizen, harmless and helpful, 'what if he is gay?'
Do you care what others do in bed, as long as they 'are not gay?'
Why condemn someone's son for the same thing because 'he is gay?

They are not criminals, thieves and cheats, 'they are just gay'
Respect them for being human don't reject them 'for being gay'
We have no right to condemn others "gay" or any other way.

Discrimination makes me angry, why judge others 'for being gay?
They contribute a lot to society, why exclude them, 'for being gay'
We don't exclude others for their looks, accept all 'straight and gay'

This morning I was reading "Out of the Shadows" by Walt Odets". This poem was born out of anger at the ill treatment, injustice and discrimination against a group of people who have done no wrong, and they can't help their sexuality any more than they can their gender and appearance, just like everybody else on this earth.

I dedicate this poem to all LGBTQ people, their families, friends and foes in this world. And I would like to remind everybody that Christ never ever mentioned homosexuality let alone condemn it. If He did, I'd like to know where it is written so that I can read it.

Esther

3 November 2019

Good Doers

To all those good doers, I have a question to ask
I hope they can give a really good answer quick fast
Why object to designer children? I should have one if I must.

They can have a son with muscular dystrophy if they want
They can also have a child with polycystic disease if they want
They can have one with many hereditary disorders if they want

I am not stopping them; I don't force my values, on them
Why do they insist on taking away my choice from me then?
Should they be allowed to stop progress? it's not up to them.

This a free country we should all have a choice, right or wrong
But we must accept the consequences of what we do farther on
You, Good Doers shut up let everyone choose, leave us alone.

Got home from work late, my mind was racing. I thought of my discussion with Elliot and how influenced he was by the 'objectors to everything' in our society. We now have the choice of having healthy children free of horrible genetic disorders. This poem was born out of anger with 'objectors' to Everything.

Esther

1/6/13

Greed

Oh, how I wish I could hug her and tell her
Just how much I really and truly love her
And point out to her the vanity of Greed
And how she surpasses by far, all need.

Put Greed on the scales and weight her
And you'll find you can not satisfy her
No matter how much she has or you give her
The more she has the more she is unhappier.

So sad, that Greed has never known it really is
More blessed to give than to receive
Because her eyes are big and only see
That her coffers are empty, though full they be.

Greed is blind to justice and to fairness
Her hunger for more she cannot harness
She will grab form rich and poor alike
Her brother, friend, kin and all she can find.

Greed, stop! Open your eyes and look around
The pain and grief, ill-gotten riches are bound

To bring to them, who others relentlessly hound,
For wealth, unjustly and ruthlessly chase around.

Dearest, if riches unfairly in this world you gain
The fire for sure will catch, and without mercy
Will burn them with pleasure and much fancy
While you struggle, to hold onto them in vain.

Remember, no matter what in this world you have
Power, riches, fame, gold, and more of the same
At your death, others will gladly inherit and claim.
But how will you stand before your God on that day?

Esther

I dedicate this poem to my niece Gia.

My philosophy in life: Pride, arrogance and jealousy destroy the soul of the person who nurses them but Greed destroys everything and everyone in her wake, it effects the whole world, and I see Greed, as the cardinal sin, the basis of all evil and suffering in the world

20 September 2019

Grey Day

A grey day always makes me feel blue
It's the same colour, just a different hue
But the difference it makes I can't tell you

I feel tired, I can't sleep I look like a sick dog
I find myself thinking sad things, I'm in a bog
Depression follows me around like a vicious dog.

Death does not frighten me, he is now my friend
Stays with me in the wakeful nights, sits on my bed
I want him to take me away, sleep in his arms no end.

How do you feel in a grey day? I will tell you more
I do not care about anything, family, friend or foe
I want to sleep peacefully, and wake up no more.

I want to be in the land with no grey days for ever more
To enjoy unending sunshine in a summer that ends no more

How I hate this seasonal depression! I can't cope any more.

I have suffered seasonal depression since I was 11 years old. I didn't recognise it as such till later in my life. I feel rotten, I feel as if death is imminent and frankly it doesn't scare me at all when I feel down. I am sure I will die late winter to mid spring, that's when I am at my lowest ebb.

Esther

5 March 2020

Happy Birthday Miranda

To my daughter

You have given me much joy and pride,
Which no money on earth can never buy.
I love you dearly, and I will, till the day I die
You have been a blessing to me all your life.

Thank you for forgiving me when criticising you harshly,
Thank you for forgiving me for dealing with you unjustly,
Thanks for accepting and treating me undeservedly gently
Thank you for forgiving me readily and so very completely

I love you, and I will die happy, knowing you have forgiven me completely

May you have a wonderful day and life on this earth.
Of all the people in this world, you deserve it most.

With all my love xoxo

Mum

5 March 2020

Happy Birthday Timothy

To my son

Your honesty and understanding are truly amazing
They surpass that of many others I'm not exaggerating
Your presence generates respect for you, and praising.

Continue to live your life helping others as you have,
May you have a wonderful day and life on this earth.
It is your reward for all you have done, this you deserve.

May you have a wonderful day and life on this earth. You brighten other people's days

With all my love xoxo

Mum

13/9/2015
Gilwell Park
Epping Forest
Chinford Essex
UK

He Loves Us All

There is only one loving God in Heaven the father of us all
He created us all in His image 'n someday He'll take us home
To a better place, with things we haven't seen or heard before

We are all His children, black, white, and yellow too
Not two of us on this earth are alike this is also true
Red is our blood, we all laugh, often we cry, yes, we do.

We feel pain 'n sorrow deep in our soul and death touches us all
We spend all our lives toiling to survive, you know it, don't you?
We all have our problems; blue blood makes no difference at all.

We fight and hate each other, it was never meant to be so
'Love one another as I loved you' He said a long time ago

This law was given to humanity, and we should keep it all.

Love unites, love is strong, love gives vigour and joy to all
Hate divides, hate destroys, hate spreads war 'n death galore
We all know it; we don't like it and together we must fight it.

And if we all join hands; we might make it.

Esther

20/7/ 2018

Her Ladyship

She sits on the couch, dolled up, laptop on her knee
Waiting for him to come home and prepare her tea
He is much delighted her pretty face and smile to see.

My Sweet Heart, I love you, what would you like for tea?
Cook whatever Darling, I don't mind, just bring it to me
Roasted chicken, vegies and ice cream, lovely would be.

I wonder what these women have, I am not endowed with?
Do they serve on a silver platter? that doesn't take much wit.
Do they flatter him? 'You are strong, wonderful, I am so weak'.

He is mesmerised, to her tune he dances, her slave he will be
His ego she strokes, won't let him know, in her net he will be
If his manhood is not threatened, his eyes won't be opened

Contended and happy for ever and ever with her he will be.

Esther

Dedicate this poem to all the smart. manipulative women on earth

Esther

19/06/2017

Humanity

We all live and we all die
We all laugh and all of us cry
We all love and we often hate

We all feel joy and more often pain
We all feel pride and often shame.
Our minds and souls are the same

We all have red blood in our veins
Our skin may be of different colour
But in every way, we are like each other

Forget religion, race and colour,
He said we must love one another
Follow His command, care for each other

Esther

1 August 2017

I Am Safe

Do fears and doubts beset you on every side?
Do you worry too much to sleep at night?
'Come to me' He said, 'your steps I will guide'.

Vicious wolfs lurk everywhere in this life
My helpless, little lambs they have in site
But my holy angels I have sent, you to guide.

I don't care about tomorrow
I know I am safe in His arms
I know His insurance is the best there was.

Esther

27/8/13

I Am Free

Lord, open my eyes that I may see
The riches of knowledge hidden in Thee
To see the great love, You have for me
Not the Law of Moses that condemns me.

Give me discernment in Your books to see,
The true, the holy, the mundane the history,
To understand that in Christ I'll always be free
His death on the cross is sufficient for me.

'I delight to do Your will' my God, this You know
I looked for it in many books and at last I saw
True Religion, helping the needy, is Your Law
In the widow's mite 'n the cheerful giver, I sure saw.

Esther

13 Nov 2019

I Changed

From the hair of my head down to my toes I have changed. I don't recognise myself now.
My hair changed from black to white, but how?

It is thin and straight, my eyelashes are gone
My eyebrows are nearly white and half fell off.
My skin is flaking 'n sagging doesn't look so hot.

My legs are shaking and look like a world map,
With blue rivers and bumpy hills all over them
My boobs hang low they look like empty sacks.

My fingers are not as nimble, they are full of knots
My joints are stiff, inflexible is it arthritis or is it not?
That's bad, but losing my sight, I cannot cope at all.

My bones have stopped growing a long time ago
But for a strange reason my skin keeps growing on
It hangs lose on my bones, doesn't look good at all.

My sense of smell is gone, and my ears don't work,
I pretend I can't hear them; do they believe me or not?
The sphincters are loose, I try hiding it but I cannot.

The noise is deafening the farts and belching smell bad
I pretend it didn't happen; try hiding it, do you think I can?
I wear a nappy, but the bloody thing is bulging in my pants.

I have told you my sad story, one more thing I want to say
Growing old and decrepit is not much fun that I will accept
Old age with her disadvantages isn't pretty but is privileged.

I am grateful for growing old, decrepit and very wrinkly
My mother died young; her children grow up didn't see
To get married 'n have children, grandchildren didn't see.

I was thinking of all the medical appointments and tests I have to attend to. They are more of them in two weeks that there have been in the last two years. This poem came about out of the realisation that I am growing old.

Esther

16 July 2018
Kalorama Vic

I Would Like

I would like a voice just like a Siren's
Sweet and melodious like an angel's
To thank God, for His love and goodness.

I would like to sing like a nightingale
To sooth my fellow man's pain away
To calm a crying child to sleep or to play.

I would like to bring sweet memories to all
Of everything they love and dearly hold on
Till this earth's sad memories, are no more.

I would also like to have a lot of money Lord
To build schools and train teachers galore
To educate many children and feed the poor.

Then the enormity of the task, slowly sinks in
I soon realise, my inability and inadequacy
And no matter how hard I try it may never be.

I really would like to fix this big, worldly mess
But who am I to think I can, I will never guess,

I become sad, disheartened, faint but tearless.

Esther

I was relaxing with Miranda after a hard day's work. She put a CD on by Andreas Bocelli. I marvelled at that beautiful voice, and once again I wished I could sing. I remembered how for a long time now I have been saying to myself 'when I get there, the first thing I will ask God, is to give me a voice sweeter and more melodious than all the angels in heaven, to sing His praises for eternity, for I, as a human have more to thank God for. I have redemption to thank Him for, the angels don't'. Put pen and paper, and the frame of this poem was formed in my mind. Wrote it in less than 45 minutes at 2:30 am.

24 5 2017

Is It You?

How sad that some people will always think that
Their cheating and lies hidden for ever they will be
They don't know, that the winds will sometime catch
And to the mountains form east to west they'll disperse.

I wish I could tell them that deception is not worth
The gain and satisfaction for a moment they will get
For with their head to the ground they'll always walk
When the one they've deceived, to them will not talk.

Think hard my dear, a question mark on you character
Don't leave, sooner or later time the truth will reveal
To shame you and your family for as long as you all live.
Please decide your old ways behind you, for ever to leave.

Life is too short in fear to live, wondering that someone might,

Our secrets one day reveal and a red mark on our name leave.
Remember? 'It is better your eye than your reputation to lose'
You will not regain it, hard as you might try, as long as you live.

I dedicate this poem to my niece Nat.

Esther

Wed 6 Sept 17

Jailed

I am in jail alone, sad and locked up
Because I was silly, and badly acted up
But my mind and soul will always be free
Jail will never succeed to lock them in.

I was jailed for being a naughty boy
But my spirit, now and always be free
To soar over mountain and deep sea
High as an eagle, I will fly, for I'm free.

I will see green fields and gentle hills
I will hear the sweet music of violins
I will feel the caressing of gentle winds
I will sing, my voice will always be free.

I still see lakes, and hear the waves of the beautiful, deep, blue sea.

Esther

I was returning home by train having visited my sister Eleni, thinking of her being locked up in the nursing home. I felt very sad. Here was a woman who loved open spaces from childhood and lived most of her life in the country. In my mind's eye, I likened her to a prisoner. I also thought of prisoners and wandered how they must feel. I would love to be able to visit and talk with them.

9 July 2018

Jemima

She is pretty, intelligent and very wise
Plans for tomorrow keeps her eye open wide
Hard working, independent, flies in the sky.
I miss her so much I wish she was nearby

My little granddaughter has grown up.
At the airport not long ago, I said goodbye
To explore the world so big, and so wide.
Time has flown so fast, I really want to cry.

I will see her soon, hug her, see her smile
hope she'll say 'I am doing well, don't worry
I will be home soon again, I will be nearby
I'll visit you often, I promise, please don't cry'

I was at Miranda's place last night, thinking of Jemima. The first verse of this poem came to my mind. I got up, penned this poem for her and went fast to sleep. Looking forward to seeing her at Christmas

16/9/13

Kids In A Playground

Like little kids in a big playground
We squabble, bicker, kick, yell 'n fight
God, we try to represent on this earth
When we don't know what He's all about.

We play His Game, His rules we think we know
We say this you must do, us you must follow,
There you must go 'n for sure you will kick a goal
We speak eloquently but tell me, what is it all about?

The assembly you must not neglect do as we say.
Is it on Friday or Saturday? No, Sunday is the day.
I'm confused, lost and frustrated can't tell you how.
The Koran? The Buddha? No, the Bible is the way.

I've read them all carefully three times over or more
I still run around like mad, there is no difference at all.
I joined the footy, the rugby, the cricket and the baseball

Their rules are different, but you're still under control.

Moses played the game well; he was a lawyer you know
He tied the loose ends safely, his laws some still follow.
'Great rewards you'll reap if you do what I've written
But beware! Cursed you are if any you have forgotten'.

All this is too hard for me, I cannot work it out.
Free I want to be in God, with rules not tied down.
I went to many clubs, sat down on many pews
So boring their sermons are, so stale their views.

A dollar I gave to a poor man once it made me feel so good
A crying woman's hand I held, by a dying man's bed I stood
Their family's grieving tears I saw, but not a word I said.
I knew well what poverty was, I knew what it was to be sad.

The voice of the Master I heard one day it was sweet and clear
'I have compassion for these people' 'they will faint I fear'.

Booth the hungry still feeds, Hollows sight to the blind gives
And when a man another helps, for sure God's Law he keeps.

Knowledge we do not need, His will to do or to know.
The 'goats' had it all in their heads, quick they were to show.
'Miracles we performed in Your name' this they pointed out
'We preached sermons for You,' this too, they let Him know.

'I don't know you and of your miracles I have never heard,
'Go away', in firmness to the hypocrites He sorrowfully said.
'Come blessed of the Father' His sheep He lovingly called
You didn't know me, but Heaven on this earth you created

Lord, now that I know what I should be and do,
Your will is clear to me, this You showed me how,
Please help me to always follow in Your footsteps
The dream You gave me long ago, help me follow.

I feel like a big, square peg in a small, round hole and I wonder if I'll ever find a place where I'll fit in and where I can worship God in spirit and in truth, just like Mary did a long time ago.

Esther

July 20014

Lawrence

You came to this world real quick
When they slammed the brakes on,
In Kensington's busiest street

'The poor little thing, he hit a post'
Said your mother in great dismay
When she saw your crooked, little nose.

'He is so long and pathetically skinny,
He looks as if he descended from spiders'
'No' said I 'he has four legs minus'.

I know a handsome boy he will be
Just wait for a little while till his hair
Grows to match his beautiful blue eyes.

He had plans, purpose and determination
Blind Freddy could see that his head was
Screwed on his neck, the right direction.

'I will work and I will study, yiayia'
He told me with great conviction
And I know he won't lose his direction,

I am happy and proud; I am tickled pink.
When I see him work hard at everything,
And the good results he always brings in.

I 'm sure he will do it with flying colours
Handsome, smart and very mature
Is my much-loved grandson, Lawrence.

Wishing you a great 20th birthday, and many more to come.

Your ever loving Yiayia xoxoxo

4 /10/ 2020

Legalise Them

Thousands of healthy, young people the world over are dying
Having no idea, not knowing what's in the drugs they are buying

While the drug lords are getting richer and powerful all the time
Living in posh suburbs, and in luxury, our young people are dying.

We know that inhibition does not work, never has, and never will
Russians sent illegal alcohol brewers to Siberia, but it stopped nil.

Churches are screaming "protect our children from the evil of drugs"
How stupid can one be! Just stop your demands and think for once.

Tell a young person all you like, "drugs you are not allowed to do"
I will put my neck on the chop, they'll defy you, the opposite will do'

Educate, educate. Tell them truthfully why drugs they should not do
Give them facts of what drugs do, let them decide which way they go.

Anyway, have you ever stopped to think who the objectors really are?
Who in our societies are the loudest objectors against legalising drugs?

I think I know, but I stand corrected, please forgive me if I am wrong
I would say with some certainty, I just about pretty well know them all.

Let's think for a moment: who makes a good living out of selling drugs?
Who is bound to be the biggest looser, if governments legalised drugs?

I am sure you don't need much thinking power to work out that one
It is of course the drug lords who control the trade, big and small ones.

Another group would be the corrupt officials in influential positions
And the "holly" ones on pulpits preaching "thou shall not do that".

We know governments make money taxing cigarettes and alcohol,
And we all know they kill more, regulate drugs and minimise harm.

They'd have us believe that drugs are bad for you, and I agree with that'
But so are cigarettes and alcohol they kill many more people than that

I am amazed at the gutlessness of governments to stand up and say,
'Pull the rug from under the feet of the drug lords we'll control the trade'!

Esther

The drug legalisation is very close to my heart, and I feel strongly about the subject. I get upset every time I hear of a young person dying of an accidental illegal substance overdose. And having lost my much-loved step grandson to accidental overdose, I get upset every time I hear of another young people dying from accidental drug over dose. None of these young people would have died if the illegal drug trade was legalised and regulated by the government as is by Enlighted European countries. Unfortunately, the drug problem discussion is still a 'Tabu' in most countries therefore citizens remain ignorant of the benefits of drug legalisation, and the ignorant ones are the loudest objectors. Illegal drugs are readily available anyway mostly in exorbitant prices at the cost of young people and the benefit of the drug lords. I will let the poem say the rest of my feelings and sentiments.

August 2 2020

Life

Life is such a cruel, nasty and unfair bitch
But she is also beautiful and very sweet.

She is full of surprises some are bitter some sweet
They come from anywhere, no warnings she gives.

When the clouds are dark and the thunder is loud
When lightning strikes and no hiding place is found

When you can't see through your bitter tears
When danger surround you filling you with fears

When you are so distressed and you want to die
When you think that the gave a good place to hide

Look up and know, it will not be for ever, the sun still shines
Behind the dark clouds, the wind will disperse let the sun shine.

The birds will sing in the trees again,
children will laugh, run and play
You will be filled with joy at the things they
say, you will laugh again.

The storm will pass, nature will be calm,
the grass will be green again.
Pain will fade, though memories remain,
but God wipes all tears away.

One day, Death will lose his sting, pain will
be no more, it will disappear
Life won't be a bitch anymore she'll be
sweet, there will be no more fear.

Esther

I received a saddening email from my granddaughter Jemima, in UK. She, amongst other employees became redundant due to covid19. I thought of all the people grieving the loss of their loved ones, the people who lost their businesses, their jobs, and their homes. I thought of the ones feeling fearful and anxious because of the uncertainty the corona virus is spreading around the world. I wrote this poem and dedicate it to Jemima and to the rest of the people effected by the virus.

14 Feb 2018

Little Girl

Another little girl came into your life
You are fortunate to see her smile
May she bring you much joy and pride
May she grow in grace 'n beauty all her life.

Esther

I was thinking of Maria, my favourite nurse and remembered that I didn't write a poem for her second little girl when she was born. This little verse came to mind. It is for Yana who is now just four years old.

March 24 2017

Little Things

A little ice cream machine I bought
And to the Lord for His blessing I brought.

My hand I asked Him fast to hold
Lest my faltering feet stumble and I fall.

Lord, big trees from little seeds grow
Bless my efforts, to You my God I call now.

This prayer came to me on my way to the shop to buy an ice cream machine to try making coconut ice cream as a money-making business to help others. One more idea of the many I had.

I wonder what is going to become of all this effort. I will not give up till all doors are closed, and I hit a brick wall

Esther

20 October 2019

Matthew

He was kind, helpful, very unselfish and generous
Intelligent, hardworking, his looks were fabulous
I have accepted he is gone the feeling is horrendous.

But I'm struggling to understand the reason why
Should a young man seeking some pleasure had to die?
Leaving the people who loved him much, every day cry.

I looked at him in shock and disbelief, shed many tears
Matthew, please get up, I'd gladly swap with you my dear
You have a job to do in Japan darling, but he could not hear.

I will always think of him in sadness. He didn't have to die, and would not, if the government had their act together and legalised and controlled the quality and strength of illegal substances. The way drugs are sold now, unregulated, will kill more and more young people who, more likely than not at some point in their life, would realise there are better ways to enjoy life and give them up. After more than 20 years since he died, the debate is still raging on, but governments are deaf, blind and stupid. When will they realise that prohibition doesn't work, has never worked, and it will never work! Wake up governments, young people's lives are far more important than the few votes of the vociferous, ignorant, objectors and religious conservatives.

June 2 2020

Mr. Trump

Mr. Trump, you might quell the unrest of the suppressed just for a little while
But you will never quell the anger and injustice which drives human kind wild
And you will never ever stop unrest, while injustice reigns in the American mind.

Don't stand holding the bible vowing to protect your friends' property, it's unwise
Fall on your knees, you and all your police, humble yourselves, that will be wise.
Apologise for crimes committed, and pain caused, it will be healing, will be kind.

Whose property are you vowing to protect? Yours, or your rich friends?' may I ask?
Are you worried about your properties and that of your cronies? take off you mask!
Are you vowing to protect the rich by quelling fairness, justice to get what you want?

Brute force controls for a while but in the end, be sure justice will always prevail
Injustice and oppression will be overcome when people are fed up, and justice crave
They will fight, shed their blood they will die unreservedly for fairness 'n justice's sake

You are threatening to bring in the national guard and the army, what the hell for?
It'd be wiser if you took a moment to look at the root of all this evil would it not?
You wouldn't have this unrest if George wasn't trodden to death, would you not?

The man was restrained and hand cuffed, he was no danger to anyone at all.
If your police did not confuse their duty, George Floyd should be taken to the law
A man on the ground helpless, facing down, a boot on his neck saying 'I can't breathe'

Teach your police their duty done humanely and with discretion not brute force
Warmth, melts the iceberg quicker than a sledge hammer and much brutal force.
Remember the ancient saying? 'A sweet tongue brings the snake out of its hole'

Mr. Trump, with your 'wisdom and enthusiasm' you are dividing America again
You don't need to be a wizard to see you are heading for a bloody civil war again
Forgive me if I am wrong, please think if you can, what you are saying may be wrong

Esther

I was watching the news again and heard Trump's threatening to quell this unrest, and "to protect you, and all you have" even if he has to bring in the national guard, the whole of the police force and the army. I felt like screaming, "you fool, all you have to do is first of all apologise and then look at the attitude of your police force and the way they treat all the American citizens. "Black and yellow red and white, they are all precious in His sight" the little children of America would gladly sing it for you I am sure of it.

14 October 2019

My Daughter

To my eyes she is beautiful and perfect in everyway
She is my treasure, brings joy and much pride my way
She is my idol; I worship her as if she is in a gold frame.

Her little hands are very deft when using a needle
Those hands are just as deft with hammer and chisel
She is capable, didn't need to be a perfectionist as well.

When I watch her adjusting a detail ever so small,
I want to scream 'it's so insignificant, leave it alone'
'Mother, if it's worth doing, do it well or not at all'.

She has a sharp eye, quickly notices the smallest fault
Points at it and says, 'mother you missed that spot'
This job is worth doing, you'll have to repaint the lot'.

My blood pressure rises I can't tell you how I feel
I don't know if it's me, or her I want to instantly kill
'No, I don't see it, it's so small, I won't do it. I feel ill.

In this world there is no absolute perfection
Striving to achieve it creates much frustration.
Near enough is good enough in every situation.

Except of course for three things: Tatts Lotto, precise engineering and if the third is not quite right, this earth would not be populated.

This poem was born out of frustration. I wish she wasn't such a perfectionist but I love her just as she is.

Esther

July 1 2019

My Mobile

Oh, how I hate that horrible little invention
I would smash it without much hesitation
It follows me everywhere, has no consideration.

It rings early in the morning, loud and clear
It rings late in the evening, gives me much fear.
It rings when I'm in the shower all bloody year.

Follows me in the kitchen, it never stops at all
Rings when I'm sleeping or sitting on the "throne"
Rings me at work, the shops I wish it would stop.

Does my head in, tries my patience makes me sin.
I would love to find its inventor and throw it at him
This little device, drives me really crazy, believe me.

Please put it in the coffin with me, six feet under

It can ring all it likes, and as loud as a thunder
It will not bother me; I'll be asleep 6 feet under.

One way or another, I'll get my sweet revenge
I might even try to bury it while I'm on this earth
It can rot, it can rust, I don't care, it can bust.

All this technology makes me feel small and stupid but the mobile phone does my head in. I sometimes wish I could turn the clock back just 30 years when we had the black, corded phones, with no answering machines, and you could decide who to ring and when.

21 August 2020

My Mother-In-Law

Who said 'a mother-in-law can never be a mother'
I loved mine, and will cherish her memories for ever

She was thoughtful as only a mother can be
Her house and heart were always open for me

I loved visiting, treated me well didn't feel discriminated
She treated me as a daughter, she was very fair minded.

She cared for my little ones with love, joy and a smile
Cleaning them was the biggest privilege one could find.

Stood at front of the stove cooking sumptuous meals for us all
Wouldn't let me help 'you go, rest', she'd say in a caring tone'

Never a word of criticism she ever uttered against me at all
She loved me unconditionally as I am, ulcers warts and all.

I have treasured memories of her, with me she will always be
I think of her as a saint, a special person, like her I want to be.

I loved her, I missed her she is now sleeping at Sale cemetery
I am looking forward to the day when we will meet some day

Esther

I was thinking of my mother-in-law and suddenly I missed her again. I thought of the kindness and care she showed my children and me. I have always counted myself privileged to have met her and to be part of the wonderful Adams family, they were hand-picked. This poem also applies to my father-in-law. I dedicate it to both of them.

26/5/13

My Prayer for Elliot

Lord, open his eyes that he may see
A better life he'd have with Thee
Lord, open his eyes that he may see
A better man that he could be
Lord, open his eyes that he may see
The blessing to all that he could be.

Lord, open his eyes that he may see
The pride and joy that he could be
To all around him, by walking with Thee.
Lord, walk beside him and gently say,
'Son, come with me, there's a better way
To spend your youth, your life, and energy'.

Lord, grant what he touches turn to gold
To ditch the drugs that destroy his soul
And waste his life, his strength his all.
Lord, he has the power by Your grace
To bust the drugs that bind and brace.

Please give him strength and the will
To be the man You'd have him be,
A blessing to friend and foe in Thee.
Lord help him unleash the gifts he has
His gentle, loving, unselfish heart,
His mind so intelligent and sharp.

Lord, how I wish that I could be
A little ray of light and help to him

To show him my love, my pain, my fear
When I think of the danger he is so near.
Lord, please help him turn his life around
To know the peace and joy that's found
By them who walk with You, safe and sound.

And Lord, if You see it fit to bring him down,
Please lift him up and give him life's crown.
I want to see before they lay me in the ground,
Just what a great man my grandson Elliot can be.
And now Lord, I want to thank You once again
For the prayers, you've answered me in the past,
And I know, I believe and I will always trust,
That this one too, You will answer me very fast.

With much love, xoxoxo

Your-ever loving yiayia

When the heart is aching, the soul finds many ways to express that pain. It may be in song, in dance in conversation or just in words uttered randomly. And in my writing this poem I have been able to accept and deal with my feelings and fears, and I find comfort every time I think of him, or I read them.

May 24 2018

My Sister

An old woman in a nursing home walks around mindless
She goes from chair to chair or stares in space motionless
She is confused and forlorn, a picture of utter loneliness.

She is looked upon as broken furniture, useless long ago.
What good is she? Her own children doesn't even know
Pulling her hair crying, 'I want to die, please let me go'.

She doesn't recognise her children, their names she forgets
The sparkle has long gone from her eyes, her soul is lifeless
Her body moves, she breathes but her spirit is emotionless

You see an old woman, toothless, dishevelled and malodorous
I see a bright-eyed little girl, energetic, intelligent and joyous
A bride, new mother, young woman, hardworking and serious.

Brings tears to my eyes, breaks my heart, why? I asked
My dear little sister is gone, I grieve, my spirit is crushed
Life is so fickle, brings joy 'n sorrow, I'll be strong, I must.

Esther

I wrote this poem having visited Eleni today. As usual I got upset, just a little more today. I wrote this poem in the train, on a tissue, on the way home.

17 Sept 2020

My Sister Carole

I have known you for a while now, my respect for you has grown over the years
No harsh, critical words I have ever heard you utter against anybody in my ears.

You only see good, virtues and strengths, not the weakness or failings in others
You have never spoken evil of anyone, I only heard you speak kindly of others.

I love you, being with you energises me, and my flagging spirit uplifts
Your gentleness, understanding and kindness, a tender chord in me touches.

God has put people like you on this earth, to show what love and kindness can do
Others to comfort, to help and to cheer, to take away their pain and ease their woe.

I lost both my sisters, I was sad, but you came along, you stand in their place now
You are my sister: you filled my empty soul you are worth ten sisters to me now.

Carole, thank you for adopting me, you'll be in my soul in their stead, always as now
I love and respect you, it's a privilege to have had you as a friend and as a sister now.

18 July 16

Myrtle Tree

I sat under the shady myrtle tree, with a hot cup of tea.
I thought of the person who planted here just for me.
I enjoyed its shade and flowers, wondering who was she.

This morning I planted a beautiful little Myrtle tree
I won't be on this earth to see it grow and big to be,
But when it flowers, someone else will enjoy and see.

Their breath will be taken away by its beauty as was for me.
Remember, we are travelling through, including you and me
The earth was given to us, to plant grass and a beautiful tree.

After us, others will enjoy the work of our hands as of others' we do
The earth is not just ours, it's for generations that'll come in time due
We must think of it as divine, given to us all, to treasure and to mind.

Esther

November 4 2019

Newborn

You came to this world looking like a cross between a hedgehog and a pug.
Your mouth looked like a fish, your cheeks were fat, you had no neck at all
You nose was flat, pushed out of shape, you looked as if it hit a telegraph pole.

Your parents looked in dismay and said "What the hell did we bring in this world?"
Later they thanked God it was only a short stage that you looked like a gnome.
You soon morphed from a caterpillar into a butterfly with beautiful curly hair on.

You grew up and blossomed, you thought you were smart that you knew it all
You thought parents were stupid, tried to teach them, they knew nothing at all
And they learned nothing, you wondered why they were so dumb, you knew all.

By the time you were 30 you thought your parents learned a thing or two
By the time you reached 40 you thought they learned as much as you knew
When you were 50, you said 'they weren't stupid, they knew more than I thought'

Horrors! They've changed, they look like
a cross between a turkey 'n an old turtle.
They have no teeth, their cheeks hang low,
they have wrinkles, their hair is gone,
They morphed from humans to gnomes
just as you did, but in reverse so long ago.

Old age comes around really fast. You look
around you once, you are married
You look again and you are old, you are a
grandparent, you're happy and proud
You look again, you are older, wrinkly
useless, decrepit, slow and grave-bound

I dedicate this poem to all the young people who don't think they'll ever grow old and who think they know it all.

Esther

Sat 12 May 2018

Norman

I lost my darling in the forest of life's many cares
I looked for him, I called him, I shed many tears
I was lonely, in agony, my cries fell on deaf ears.

I lived with him but was alone and in much fear,
I told him of my pain, 'all's well' he said 'I'm here'
'No, when I talk, you do not listen, see, nor hear'.

I struggled, I wept and plead with him for three years
I prayed and waited for him, to open his eyes and ears
All in vain, he was oblivious, ignored my fears and tears.

'Lord, what will I do? I'm suffering alone, he doesn't care
I will pack my things and run far away, but not this year
My children are still at home, they need me, I'll be near.

Esther

25 May 2021

Ode To A Tree

The seasons came and the seasons went
And that beautiful tree across the road
Changed its garb from green to bright red.

I love that stately mountain Ash tree,
It shades the house that's build under it
From the searing, scorching summer heat.

It lets the winter sun get in, brightens it
Warms every corner and the people in it
Its branches are bare again, big and gaunt'

The shadows it throws on the house are long
They are weird and complicated they haunt
But soon It'll be dressed in lush green as before.

 I will wonder at its beauty; I will admire it and I will hush.

I was sitting up in bed working at the computer, and lifted my eyes for a rest. I looked across the road at the mountain Ash tree, at which I have been looking for the last two and a half years admiring it. I wrote this poem in its praise and the countless other trees which brighten our lives and which we take for granted.

24 July 2019

Old Age

I don't know what's happening to me
I laugh and I fart, I cough and I pee,
What is the next thing going to be?

My ears aren't working they buzz continuously
My eyes are funny, without glasses double I see
My bones are cricking, lose my balance constantly

My neck is stiff, my hands are very weak
I drop everything, my toes I cannot feel
My feet and shins tingle, up to my knee

Doctor, doctor, tell me what's happening to me?
'Don't worry dear, it won't go above your knee
Can't do much about, it it's peripheral neuropathy'.

'Many people over 65 suffer from this disease'.
I was not comforted, I was not very pleased
OK for him to be blaze but he's talking about me.

My skin is flaking, my hair is limp and very thin
My spine is curving, my head is touching my knee
I have more waddles on my neck than an old turkey.

The whole system is out of order, repairs I need
A plumber to fix the sphincters so they don't leak
Someone to stretch the gullet so I don't choke on tea.

Where are all the experts? Can anyone help me?
To cure the arthritis and replace that wonky knee.
To take my woes away and make a brand new me.

I don't recognise this old woman, where is the real me?

This poem was born out of embarrassment. I was talking to the concreter and his wife. He said something funny, I laughed and farted. I thought 'if I heard it, they must have heard too. I was mortified. When I went to bed later, and couldn't sleep, I remembered the incident. I sat up in bed and wrote this poem in less than an hour. Old age is not pretty but she is certainly very privileged. I thank God every day for the privilege of growing old.

23 August 2018

Old Lady

A little old lady, sprayed herself and well perfumed
To the toilet she ran but unfortunately, she missed
On herself and on the floor, she accidentally pissed.

Poor dear, for the perfume bottle she quickly reached
The smell of the piss she tried with all her might to beat
Sprayed well, she didn't know in her slippers she pissed.

'Mother dear, a refreshing shower I think you might need'
'I am washed well, a clean outfit I certainly don't need'
Yourself you are smelling; I am fresh and well perfumed.

This poem came to mind, when gardening. I had to run to the bathroom. I made I it just on time. I wondered if this would always be the case, or if there would come a time when I wouldn't make it. I realised that if I lived long enough there would come a time, when I too, like the rest of humanity would either piss myself, wear a diaper as well as a bib: not a very flattering thought, but they do say 'We start with a diaper and a bib and we end up with a diaper and a bib'.

18/03/2015

Pearls Of Wisdom

I woke up thinking about my conversation with Miranda last night and a little Greek adage about relationships came to my mind. I thought about it and translated from Greek it goes something like this.

A son-in-law, a son can never be
Neither a daughter-in-law a daughter
Harder still to be is a mother-in-law a mother.

As I was thinking about the relationship between step parents and step children, I came up with this little 'pearl of wisdom'.

You might love and cherish your stepchild
But yours will never be, try as you might
Things change very quickly after the first fight.

Esther

24 May 2020

Poverty

Everybody knows the meaning of the word, but not all understand
The feeling of unworthiness, and suffering when poverty is at hand.

The pangs of hunger, the winter's bitter cold that chills you to the bone
The unbearable heat in the unlined tin shed, is hot as hell, but it's home

The dejection, helplessness, and injustice in the 'haves and have nots'
You live in a slum, no running water, no place to privately take a wash

You gather sticks to cook a paltry meal for you and your loved ones
While a mile farther up, others live luxuriously in houses built of bricks.

You dream the impossible dream, for a better future life, and all that
Ask me, I know how it all feels, I experienced it, I'm familiar with that

But remember, if you can dream it, you can achieve it if you work hard

> Never give up, focus on your dream, believe in yourself and in God trust.

Esther

I woke up feeling down and annoyed as the tradesman didn't turn up today again. No matter in which room I look in, not one is finished completely. I feel depressed and dejected.

My mind raced all over the earth again and for some reason it took me back to Greece. I thought of the civil war, living in a shed, grandma cooking on bricks gathering sticks making a fire to cook us a meal. I thought of my mother's untimely death, living in a shack, no amenities for a wash in private, let alone a shower. I thanked God again as usual for all my blessings.

Suddenly and with much force it hit me that I was mocking God. Here I was feeling depressed and dejected because the house isn't finished yet! I felt ashamed of myself. I thanked God again, this time fully appreciating my good fortune and all the blessings He has so abundantly bestowed upon my family and me. I thought of the millions of people all over this earth who still live under the same conditions

This thought was enough to lift me out of the dull drums and stop me from complaining. I started writing the first two verses of this poem and finished it a couple of days later. I will not complain again about the state of the house and hopefully I will not get frustrated. And if you feel hard done by, read my autobiography ' but I Promised God' by M Koutsada.

Aug 22 2019

Precious Things

As I grow older, the glories of this earth fade away faster
I see concrete and rocks just as valuable as alabaster
The rubies and diamonds of this world lose their lustre.

If all precious stones disappeared it wouldn't be a disaster
I bought China and silver, they created so much clutter.
I carted them over air and sea, they became my master.

I don't care about them now, if they break, I don't fluster
They have no power over me, now I am their master
I look upon them now as valueless, they don't matter.

I get up in the morning wondering about this hustle and bustle
I say to myself 'slow down, you'll get to you grave much faster
We know that earthly things don't last for ever, they don't matter.

I was packing Miranda's crockery and glassware out of the cupboard. There seemed to be no end of it. I thought back at the time when I too was buying things like that, thinking they were the most necessary things in my life. Now they are not. It is amazing how our values change as we grow older.

Esther

7 12 2019

Pride

'The proud and the arrogant I hate', said the Lord.
'The nations are like dust on the scales' also said God.
If that is so, then I must be less than dust, am I not?

Riches and power are ephemeral as we are, it's our lot
On this earth they are desirable, in the grave they 're not
Being caring now is better, than rich underground is it not?

I want to help my fellow man now; with all I have got.
We can't take anything to our grave, you'd agree, not?
I want to put all I have in God's store house, little or a lot

"Love your neighbour as yourself" he said a long time ago
He did not mean you must be in love with him certainly not
I don't like lots of things about myself and proud I am not.

But I still take care of me: when thirsty and hungry I feed me,
When I'm cold I dress me, when I do wrong, I often justify me
That is my duty to my neighbour that's all God is asking of me.

I am glad He didn't say: 'Love your neighbour as your family'
That would be very hard to do, and nigh impossible humanly
He said, 'he who cares not for his own is worse than an infidel'.

Esther
This poem was born out of strong fear and dislike for arrogance and pride

3 November 2019

Psych Hospital

One is manic, dances, claps and loudly sings
One is delusional, controls the sun and winds
One is scared of his shadow yells and screams.

One is an engineer, says drills holes on the earth
To drain the flood waters from all of Queensland
He can save people and animals from drowning.

One wraps a sheet around him says he is prophet Joel
One wears a turban, he is an Indian king, he controls all
Another says he is Jesus; he can feed the whole world'

One sees shadows of dreadful devils in his room
He also sees the antichrist, he predicts a gloom
I'm confused, who the hell am I? I think I'm a prune.

What on earth possessed me to become a psychiatric nurse?
Mental illness saddens me but I like working here nevertheless
And after 40 long years I still like working in this very sad mess.

Esther

11 Feb 2020

Racism

EGW said: 'of all the evils in the world, Slavery God hates most'.
I'd say racism is just as bad. Breaks the spirit destroys the soul
Dehumanises, drags a person down, below the level of a dog.

Racism is evil, humiliates, makes me sad, mad, angry and horrible
Do I need to change the colour of my skin, to you to be acceptable?
Must I have money and degrees so that to you I can be adorable?

I look for a kind heart and a generous spirit, to me only that counts.
The colour of our skin, our garb, and background to nothing amounts
I see another human, I don't see a race, don't ask for his background.

Look deep in his soul, you might be surprised at what you have found
Another person who might need you, don't kick him to the ground.
Remember under our skin we are all the same, white yellow or brown.

Prejudice blinds, we can't see strengths of character or that of weakness
Ban it from your mind, you will be much be happier, to this I can witness
You will find a friend, you'll see a smile, you'll be richer by this experience.

Esther

A few years ago, I was sitting outside a supermarket in Footscray next to a white lady chatting while resting. A lady went by, wearing a hijab just her eyes showing. The lady next to me stopped mid-sentence, pointed to the woman and said derisively, 'look at her, look at what she is wearing, she thinks she is pleasing God!' I ignored her and when the lady went past us, I looked at the woman next to me straight in the eye, and calmly I said 'Yes, and she is praying to the same God you are praying to'. If looks could kill, I would be instantly dead. Her eyes were like daggers. She sat silently for a few moments, got up and left without event saying good bye.

That incident stayed with me for many years, and is still with me. I cannot understand the prejudice and hatred of that woman towards another person who did her no harm, she was only dressed differently.

This poem was born out of sadness because of ignorance and prejudice. I dedicate it to all the prejudiced people in the world, regardless of their race or colour.

May 5 2019

Red

'Wear something red' when she was alive always said she
It's a beautiful colour; brightens my day, it brings joy to me.
It makes me happy, I feel alive, when the red colour I see.

I had a red patch in my garden where I sat to drink my tea
My soul was uplifted, was in heaven with red colour near me
It brightened my day when a perfumed, red rose I would see.

You can sing my praises all you like, a saint certainly I was not
But I always tried to do the very best I could, that was all.
I hope they will say 'she was not perfect, she tried, that's all.

Someday, I will stand before God and will say
'Lord, a chief of sinners I was, this I already know
But His wounded hands to me He hasten to show'.

'Father, I'm covered with His righteousness' white robe
And for His sake You will have to accept me as I am now
He is here, standing by my side now, holding me close,
You cannot say 'No' now.

Esther

16 Jun 2020

Resurrection

"Resurrections" how can this incredible wonder be?
My mind boggles thinking about it, how will it be?

Lord, I know you said it a very long time ago
You proved it to be true, I'm wondering how

The only son of the poor widow on the way to his grave
The 12-year-old daughter of the Roman, dead in her bed

Lazarus dead three days in the sepulchre already decaying
Your human heart was touched by their loved ones' pain.

You did not discriminate between rich and poor
Your heart went out in sympathy to them all

You stopped the procession; did you look up saying 'Rise'?
Did you connect with the Father again, as did all the wise?

Lord, I know all this, I believe, I have heard it all before
But my finite mind gets boggled at the wonder of it all.

Do You have a little box to keep our DNA in for evermore?
We keep DNA safely, in a glass jar for eight years or more.

We create beautiful babies in a glass tube years after the event
We cloned "Dolly" the sheep. 'It's unethical' the objectors said.

We create teeth on the computer to cap our decaying ones
Soon we'll have plastic organs to replace the worn-out ones.

I can only think that You keep our DNA somewhere high up'
With our life record, to call us to life immortal when time is up.

If we, mere humans do all that, it's not hard for You to raise us up
And to recreate our human frame. I believe, I'm waiting looking up'

Esther

I was watching the news yesterday when I heard them say, they caught the serial killer of the three young women he killed eight years ago, they identifying him by his DNA.

That kept me thinking. My mind went back to Sabbath School at the North Fitzroy church discussing the subject of resurrection and how these same bodies will be raised incorruptible to live for ever more. I asked the teacher, Paul C. what happens to those people burned on the stake or the ones thrown to the lions by the Romans and watched them as sport, while being torn and eaten by the beasts. Paul had no answer. He asked me how I thought it would happen. I had no answer either, other than to say, by our DNA and our life record. I don't understand it but the DNA theory keeps me from wondering and awake at night.

March 30 2019

Revenge

Revenge is sweet to the mouth and the tongue
But when digested is very poisonous to the blood
And nothing is gained by revenge in the long run.

Yourself you are hurting more; you sadden your heart.
Enemies you make, can't sleep even when trying hard.
Forgive, you will find peace, you cannot argue with that.

'Forgive as you have been forgiven', said Jesus once
Works for all of us, on earth, and in the heaven above
Forgiving, benefits you more, believe it, but it's hard.

Esther

I was watching the young girl I was looking after, misbehave in the ward, spilling water and rubbish on the floor, for not getting a cigarette. I thought to myself this is her revenge for not getting her way. As I thought of her behaviour, I realised that some people are vengeful by nature, others are not. Hospitals are smoke free now, no one is allowed to smoke but not everybody gets revenge by throwing water and rubbish on the floor. This poem was born out of sadness and anger.

1 May 2021

Shame

1. Please mum, please don't make me feel ashamed,
Makes me feel worthless destroys my soul and mind

2 Please don't make feel guilty either it's hard to bear
It too, destroys my soul, it isn't kind, it's cruel, it's unfair.

3. I am trying so very, very hard a good little girl to be
But there is always something in my way that trips me.

4. Just tell me kindly, what I just did, or say, was wrong
I will try to remember, do it better next time and get on.

I woke up at 4am. made me a cup of tea and back to bed. My mind raced all over the earth and ended in Yallourn, over 50 years ago when Miranda was a little girl about 5 years old. With what I told her I made her feel ashamed. She put her head down, the expression on her little face one of devastation. It gave some satisfaction then, thinking that I corrected her. Now my heart is aching. I hope she can forgive me.

I wrote this poem in 10 minutes and dedicate it to her with all my love.

Mum

9 August 2020

Sobering

One foot on a banana skin, which has gone brown
The other in a six-foot, deep hole deep in the ground

I don't need money; I'm telling you now
As I am racing ahead, I am grave bound

There are no banks to invest and make heaps
There are no worries there, one just sleeps

I don't need money or riches I am telling you again
There are no shops to buy things deep under there

I have no idea what's like but I reckon it is good
It's like an anaesthetic, the pain is gone feels good

This applies to all of us, young and old alike
Death doesn't discriminate, takes us all alike

Esther

I am still suffering the effects of the winter blues and the lock-down of the corona virus, I feel down. All I want to do is curl up in a corner and sleep. Hopefully in a few weeks when the sun shines the blossoms are out and the trees are green, I will be writing happier poems

17 July 2016

Speak Not

Please speak not to the corps that's lying in this box
For you know very well that I am not in there.
Look to the clouds where my spirit rides, free as the air.

Where for a while the infinite universe it will explore,
Till the day the Lord says 'I will now to the earth will go
To take back those who loved Me and bring them home'.

I lived my life as you would all know, in joy and pain
Just like all others on this earth, we are all the same
But now I'm free from all that and with gladness I say

That one day soon, we will certainly meet again,
When our bodies and spirits will be joined again
And on the earth made new, we will for ever reign.

Now with Jesus I say 'Father to Thee I commit my spirit' today'
Accept it and keep it with my life record till that glorious day
When the books in heaven are opened and You find me worthy,

To be with You, on the earth made new and live with You for ever again.

Esther

I don't know why I wrote this poem. I think I might have been starting to feel the effects of seasonal depression.

18 August 2020

Spring

The sun is shining brightly, the birds are happy singing
They are collecting sticks and wool, nests are building

The blossoms are out, the trees green garb are wearing
The bees are buzzing, collecting nectar, honey are making

The days are long, the soil is soft and ready to work on
I want to feel the dirt on my hands, see plants grow on

Nature is awaking, bears are stretching for food are searching
My spirits are high, life is sweet, my spirit to the hills is flying

Gone are dark days, all is bright, the black clouds, are no more
Gone is sadness, a gazelle is born in green pastures we'll romp on

Let's celebrate with nature before she sleeps again all winter long

Let's soak in the sunshine that lifts the spirit and warms the bones

Esther

It is a beautiful sunny morning, more Spring than winter. Looking out the window I felt cheerful. I thought Spring is only two weeks awake we will have more days like this one, we will be able to go outside and do some gardening. Just the thought of it made me feel glad. This poem is an expression of the gladness I felt.

23 Feb 2020

The Beggar

He is sitting in the corner to keep warm, out of the wind and rain
he looks older than his years he is dishevelled very thin and wane
People go past him; some help him others look at him with disdain.

He is a mother's much-loved son who some time ago, went astray
'I thought I could easily give up drugs, but it gets harder every day.
I despise myself, I hit rock bottom, I'm lonely, my friends ran away'.

'I'm homeless, friendless, death would better than living this way'.
'I know, you have hit bottom but if you want to, you can rise again'.
'I don't know where to start from, I'm confused I can't find my way'.

'I know you are confused and lost but there is Someone up there
Who is waiting for you to stretch your hand, He will lead the way.
The Father is watching and waiting for you, get up, be on your way'.

He will throw a party for family and friends,
will celebrate with joy.
He will put a gold ring on your finger, He
will throw your rags away.
His voice will sound in the universe,
'rejoice, my son is home again!

John, this is only a parable, your parents
and friends will rejoice too
Take my hand, together, holding each
other up we'll make it through
Others took the wrong turn, but now they
have found their way too.

Get up, it's not going to be easy but
together we will find the way.
Believe in yourself, take the first step, and
we will be home again
To celebrate with your family and friends,
will be a wonderful day.

I was thinking of the young man who was sitting in a corner at the shopping centre. I'd stop and chat with him and share a bit of chicken or a bread roll. One day he told me his life story and how he had hit rock bottom. He is now homeless, penniless and depressed. I suggested he takes himself to the hospital where they can treat his depression and hopefully find him accommodation and then, he can look for a job, he said would like to work again.

This poem is dedicated to him and to the countless young people who have been caught up in the drug epidemic. I hope and pray they will find their way back to success and happiness.

Sat 30 May 2020

I saw John 2 weeks ago. He looked ever so much better. He said he connected with his brother and he is soon going to see his parents. I was thrilled for him, and for his patents. I wish I could have shared his parents' joy. I hope he does something with his life.

July 27 2020

I am very glad to say I haven't seen John again. I wish him the very best of everything in life.

Esther

23 May 2021

The Cross

'On a hill far away' Jesus walked rejected and alone all the way
Carrying my wrong doings and shame on his shoulders all the way.

He was hung on that tree, and was crucified there instead of me
His hands were nailed on that roughly hewn tree, just to save me.

They shouted and screamed in fury: crucify Him! crucify Him!
'Better one man dies, than a whole nation perish' crucify Him.

It was decreed from the beginning that You, the sinless one
The innocent Lamb of God would die in shame to save everyone.

You could have let me suffer the results of my sin big and small
But instead, you took up my cross and walked up that hill all alone.

Your pain I cannot comprehend, You suffered for all including me
You were judged in my place, You silently accepted the guilty plea.

For guilty I was in the Father's sight, I know it, I could not deny that,
But Your love for a lost world surpassed suffering, shame and all that.

Jesus, I want to be like You, forgiving the wrongs and injustices
Others have done to me, wittingly or otherwise imposed on me

Help me say, 'Father, help me forgive them all, as You forgave me.
You are the great Judge of all, You freely forgave us all including me.

I was in bed resting holding the little cross hanging around my neck from a gold chain. From somewhere in the far distant past, my father-in-law's sweet voice came to my ears singing with much feeling, 'On a hill far away, stood an old rugged cross' I sat outside in the sun and penned this poem in less than 30 minutes. I too love that cross of pain, shame and great love, which I will never fully comprehend while on this earth.

4/8/13

The Same Way Lord

This epic is the basis of my autobiography,
'...but I promised God'
1. I came to this world with a guardian angel as you'd know
I don't know what his name is, but one day I will find out
Face to face I'll see him then 'n my gratitude to him I'll show
Many times, my life he saved, that close to death I came, I know.

2. Life wasn't easy for me; dreadful things I saw 'n heard
The bitter fighting in the home, the blow of the fist I heard
My mother's cries I still hear, grandma's dismay I still see
Grandpa beat nan black 'n blue, dad tried better than him to be.

3. Dad lost all his money gambling 'n drunk came home one night
He didn't need an excuse his fury and anger to vent with all his might
'Dear what's the problem?' he was only asked 'tell us we'll try to help'
Profanities came out of his mouth, such words in my life I hadn't heard

4.His anger 'n fury knew new no bounds, someone he wanted to hurt
A knife he took from the drawer and viciously the heater attacked
Fear and dread paralysed me; the house I thought would be burned
Quickly the hot coals mum 'n nan shovelled up, the house didn't burn.

5.My cousin and my little friends to school went before me
They had a bag made of cloth, a beautiful book and a pencil
'I want to go to school too' I said to my mum, 'next year' said she
'But I want to learn to read and write' she taught me under a tree.

6.Next year took a long time to come, but it mattered not at all
Because the readers from grade one to six I had read them all.
First day at school, a dream I thought I was in, but a dream it was not
In cloud nine I was for weeks, this school business I thought was hot.

7.The year ended with a big bang, celebrations, songs, dance 'n all
Our certificates we were given with our marks and achievements on.
My mother's face beamed with pride and grandma smiled, oh, so
'Goodness' my mother said with delight 'child you 've beat them all!'

8. School couldn't start soon enough, three months away was too long
Back to school I wanted to go, more books I wanted to explore.
September came at long last, twenty-two they said we would start
But alas! I was too young to know that long it would not last.

9. Tanks and trucks and uniformed soldiers to the village arrived galore
They were all worried, 'what's going to happen? There's going to be a war'.
I wasn't worried, too young to know that death 'n pain would be the result.
Young George was the first to die,' shrapnel' they said, there were more.

10. 'The school won't open they said 'to the other village the children send'
This was easier said than done 'the river in winter floods' the parents said.
Why can't I go to school in Tsakos?' I asked 'You'll drown; you'll be dead'
The bridge was narrow, rickety too, the boards were rotten no rails it had.

11. My father by force they took out of his hiding place in the straw
'I'm too old to carry a gun, my time in the army I have served before'
'Get out, get ready, with us you are coming, even if you're forty-four
A farrier you are we're told, the horses and mules you'll to take care of.

12. The grim day came 'all the villages soon empty will be' the soldiers said.
So much confusion 'where shall we go?'
'Over the border or the city' they said
'Ten days we have to work out what to do' my mother to grandma said.
'Too risky in winter the mountains to cross, to the city we'll go' they decided.

13. Adults had their worries and problems; children had their own too
'I don't want to go away; I'll miss Toula', crying 5-year-old Gloria said.
A soldier held her in his arms, 'you will be back, the war will soon end'.
The sad truth was, she never saw her friend again, nor I my sweet heart.

14. Women worked day 'n night, no men left in the village to help
Everything on the bullock cart went, mattresses, chattels grain 'n all
Never such traffic up and down on that dirt road had I seen before
Scared, by the cart I walked, my foot under the wheel was caught.

15 No time to cry, no time attention to seek, of that sure I was
When on the cart they wanted to put on,' no' I said 'I will walk'
Extra weight I'd be, the animals struggled to pull the cart as it was
Four kilometres limping I walked; the gate to town was already shut.

16 'What shall we do?' grandma wailed 'oh how I wish I knew!'
But my forward-thinking mother the problem had foreseen
To the 'special box' she went 'n two silk scarves out of it she drew
Under the soldier's arm discreetly slid 'n whispered 'please let us in'.

17 The gun over his shoulder flung, to the gate I saw him walk
Unleashed the flimsy wire gate and 'Quickly' he said 'Get in'
On the rump of the cows the whip my mother lightly flipped
They took off hurriedly as if our fear and urgency they had seen.

18 In the razor wire surrounded town at last we were safely in
They looked around in dismay 'but where shall we sleep?'
The mid November night was cold, cloudy 'n threatening
But nowhere to go; 'the town is dark and sleeping, this is it!'

19 Mattresses and blankets on the cold ground they spread
'Get in your beds quickly, clothes, shoes and all' they said.
I don't know what the others did; blankets were over my head.
To keep out the wind was easy enough, but not so the sleet.

20 I trembled from fear and cold. 'Get up, to the shed you can go'
The young soldier's voice was caring, kind and music like soft
The mattresses were rolled over quickly; did he help? I don't know.
In the open fronted machinery shed that night we slept, but it had a top!

21. They thanked the young soldier with tears in their eyes, but he moved on.
They thanked God with all their hearts for shelter, food and protection.
No sooner it was light they got us up 'hurry' they said 'we must move on'.
A room mum found in town with two families, kids slept under beds not on.

22 And of my beautiful puppy Irma, what can I really say?
She was as cute as button; I played with her all day.
Tears still roll down my face, my little Irma was left behind
Alone, in the deserted village, her own food she had to find.

23 A mother's love for her offspring whether human or dog
Is stronger than fear, pain, hunger and much, much more
She would not abandon her puppies for anyone's affection
She stayed in the empty village, they all died of starvation.

24. To the city we moved, in church at midnight they unloaded the truck.
My mother stayed behind, the cattle to sell, and other things to fix.
Two other refugee families were there with two small beautiful kids,
Their father opened the locked steel, heavy, gate, for us to get in.

25 Life wasn't easy for any of us in that unforgettable place
The minister had no kids and cruel he was, he didn't understand
Mercilessly he beat 3yo Eleni for jumping on the rolled-up tent
Gloria, he belted for talking to the dog, and scribbling on the cement.

26 To school we didn't go that year, the teacher said 'too late to start'
'Next year will be better' grandma said, we'll make a new start.
Next year we went to school alright, but soon home we were sent
'Scabies 'n lice they have, home they must stay' the teacher said.

27 A job in the city my mother couldn't find, she worked far away on a farm.
She cleaned 'n scrubbed 'n cooked for sixty workers, oh, she worked so hard
Three years she worked in that place, we saw her every three months
No rights she had that she could call upon, she took 'whatever comes.'

28 The years passed the war raged on, home we stayed to school we didn't go.
At long last the day came 'to school you will go this year' grandma said,
She came to school with us that day, our story to the teachers she had to tell.
I was scared 'n excited, books to read, stories to hear and friends to make.

29 In grade 3 the old one will be, in grade 1 the younger', the headmaster said.
The bell rang for our classes to go, my heart missed a beat,' it's time for the test'.
In class at front of fifty kids I stood, a book was put in my hands 'read aloud'
In a harsh voice, the teacher said. I looked quickly, her face in concrete was set.

30 Fear seized me I trembled 'n shook, I looked at the book but I could not read.
Dead silence followed, all eyes were on me, the teacher fiddled with the stick.
I panicked I gulped, with tears I choked, I tried hard but not a word could I read.
She looked at me with disdain, her face and name I won't forget as long as I live.

31 Gounari was her name 'n this she said for all the class to hear, not just to me.
'You In grade 3? Who said so? In grade 1 you should start; you might cope there'
She carelessly pointed with her stick for me to sit, I felt unworthy being there.
School wasn't easy for us; we tried hard with city kids to fit in, and like them to be.

32 We tried very hard their ways to learn as well as count, write and read.
Despite the fear of the war 'n the upheaval, 'good kids' they said we were.
We finished school, we learned to read, and better marks we got than the rest
Gloria at 14 in a factory worked 'n to a seamstress the trade to learn I was sent.

33 A bigger shock we couldn't have, when my mother died at forty-three
From work to hospital she was taken, 'n home for Xmas she wouldn't be.
Three young girls she left in the city to build a house to make a home.
Teenagers we were fourteen to nineteen, but He didn't leave us alone.

34 To my cousin John and the neighbours grateful we'll always be,
A small house they built for us, we the brickies' labourers had to be.
The house was built in four days by deft hands and willing hearts
How many friends you have you'll never know, until you are in need.

35 My childhood dream was fulfilled, as an assisted migrant I signed in,
On Australian soil I landed, 'what a beautiful place, I thought this is!'
I fell in love with this land; 'my God, flowing with milk and honey she is'
I want to live and die in this land, please burry me under a coolabah tree.

36 I worked 'n studied, 'n kids I had two, after 18 years my divorce came through
Sad it was, our arguments were small, but in the end, I didn't know Norman at all.
Two different people we became, life's experiences and years changed us both
I was only thirty-six, would I stay, or would I go? With much sadness, I left it all.

37 And of my second husband, what can I really say? I've learned a lot.
Arrogance dressed well will fool you, Confidence she masquerades as.
A stingy man's trembling hands as he gives his money, you soon get to tell,
The parable of the rich man's fate 'tonight you will die' they never learn.

38 Life with all her ups and downs, has been very good to me
Not a day of all my life would I swap, nor would I refuse to re-live
Precious lessons you learn from sorrows 'n if you want, you'll see
That Sorrow with all her harshness a better teacher than Joy will be.

> I walked a mile with Pleasure
> She chatted all the way
> But I was non-the wiser
> For all she had to say.
>
> I walked a mile with Sorrow
> And ne'er a word said she

> But, oh! The things I learned from her
> When Sorrow, walked with me.
>
> Robert B Hamilton

I was out in the garden reflecting while I was walking around today and suddenly the nearness and reality of my mortality hit me with much force just as reality has a habit of doing. Went inside and penned what I think will be the last verses of my life story.

> 39 And then one day at the end of life's long journey,
> Tired, worn out and old, my God I met in a dark valley.
> 'Hello' He said cheerfully 'where are you headed for today?'
> I looked up with tears of joy, 'I'm coming home to You,' said I.
>
> 40 My loved ones I leave behind, hard thing to do, please keep them safe,
> My work is finished on this Earth I'm coming home to You today'.
> He lovingly took my hand and softly to me He whispered, 'I know,
> 'Your journey wasn't easy on this earth, but with you I walked all the way'.
>
> 41 Thank you Lord, for holding my hand and leading me on….'
> 'But wait, a deal I wand to make with you, I haven't finished yet.'
> I looked up expectantly and curious to hear what He had to say.

'One more lifetime I give you, you choose the way once again'.

42 'Another lifetime or ten more, please take my hand and lead me on
The same road, the same track we'll walk together all the way once again.
We walked in sunshine and in rain, and in many a storm we soldiered on.
On rocks, I didn't dash my foot; in Your Arms You carried me all the way.

43 The same way Lord, yes, I would walk with You again
The same road I'd tread with You for I have learned a lot.
And I know You will carry me in Your arms when the trot gets hot
Just as You did when we walked together, so long, long ago.

Esther

30 Sep 2019

The Servant Nurse

The sick Indian patient said "I found a servant"
He was grandiose, the nurse was as kind as ever
Tended to his needs fearful of him losing his temper.

He is sick, out of touch with reality he'll get better
He will apologise he will hug, and me he will pamper
'I am sorry I have been so painful I am now better'.

His mother visited, brought clothes, delicacies and the rest
Tended to him tenderly, and lovingly she did her very best
On his bed she sat, 'n expertly his feet massaged 'n caressed.

With sadness in her heart the ward she left, home she went
Her much loved son, to the nurses she left to care for 'n attend
With pleading eyes, 'n unspoken plea, said 'please do your best'.

Her son improved, and his true colours very soon emerged
He was handsome, polite, intelligent, kind and well educated
The nurse went to his room dutifully, on his welfare checked'

'Come in' he said with great authority, 'sit on my bed'
'I can't, on other patients I must also check but I'll return
His eye flashed with anger 'sit down right now' he ordered.

'Rub my feet' demanded peremptorily. 'I'm not a masseur' she said
'Rub my feet as my mother did'. 'I am ordering you' he demanded
The nurse's human nature and weakness very quickly emerged.

Her eyes in anger flashed 'I am not your mother, I'm your nurse'.
As psychiatric nurses, we take much physical and emotional abuse
We are dealing with very sick people arguing with them is of no use

But humiliation is very hard to take, we should not, it's abuse.

Esther

31/03/16

The Tooth Fairy

Abracadabra listen to me Fairy Debra,
This letter I send in the clouds today
Because Cooper's tooth you took away.
Please go to his house when he's asleep
And a gold coin under his pillow slip,
Because I know he is a good little boy
And when he says he will be very good,
I am sure his promise he'll always keep.

Esther

Dear Cooper,

I have sent this letter to Miss Fairy Debra, and because she is magical she came to my house last night and left this little present for you. She said you will have a brand new tooth in no time, but you must clean in it well, because the new tooth will only grow once. So, take good care of it. I am sure you don't want a gap between your teeth when you grow up.

Best wishes on your birthday

Esther
Love you lots xoxoxo

10 Nov 20018

Timothy

You are loving, kind and honest beyond all measure
Thinking of you gives me much pride and pleasure
By your actions and life, you live up to your name
You honour God and He honours you just the same.

Helping others to you is not a duty it is a pleasure
You do to others as you'd want them to do to you.
You are much loved, foes you might have but a few
You are thoughtful and loving, and we all love you.

Even as a child, there was no deceit in your mind
People who know you well, love you far and wide.
From Australia to Saudi, the Air Force far and nearby.
The way you live, makes my heart bubble with pride

You are a man after God's own heart, you have no guile

May you continue to grow in love 'n wisdom all the while
May He bless you and your family for the rest of your life
May life be kind to you and yours I pray now and always.

I was thinking of Timothy and the incident when he damaged the mirror of an expensive car while reversing out of a tight parking spot. Timothy wrote a note of apology with his details on it, and left it under the wind screen wiper. The owner rang later to verify that he was the one who caused the damage. Timothy owned up to it. The owner thanked him and hung up. Timothy never heard from the owner again nor the Insurance Company. As a 6-year-old he found a $10.00 note on the floor of a large supermarket in Sale. He handed it to the nearest employee. I thought again of the time he volunteered to help George renovate his sister's house. Timothy was up in the roof. He found a large bunch of money. When he came down from the roof, he gave it to Nell, I told him he should have kept it. 'No mum' it is rightfully hers' he said. She didn't give him a sent as a reward for his honesty and he never accepted payment.

He is a better man than me and many others, I am proud of him and humbled by his honesty, he doesn't need to go to church, he practices Jesus' command, 'do unto others as you would have them do to you'

Fri 7 Feb 2019

Tired

Lord, I think it is time for me to rest now, is it not?
Give me courage, to let the bird out of the cage go
It's small, restricting, I can't stretch my wings, it's hot.
I really want to go, I am tired but how, I do not know.

I want to be free from this earth's dreadful fear and pain
I want to wander in the Universe, to explore every plain
Till the day I find rest on the earth made new once again,
Where I will meet my ancestors and loved ones again.

I lived a long and satisfying life, hard sometimes it was
I tried hard, I did the best I knew how, You know that.
The suffering of my fellow man is getting me down
Spare me the indignity of infirmity I want to go now.

Esther

I started writing the first verse of this poem in Melton. I was feeling hot, tired and bothered. I wanted to rest for a while, but I had so much to do, I was overwhelmed. The heat and high humidity were suffocating, I thought I would die. I then thought to myself, this wouldn't be a bad thing really, I do want to die before I lose my independence. I started writing this poem but the electrician came and put an end to it. I forgot about it till I got in the car and was rummaging in my bag for the hospital keys. I found the cardboard piece I started the first verse on. At work, before hand-over, while the others were talking, I wrote the last two verses at the back of a tissue box.

21/4/2015

To Jemima

When dark clouds cover the whole sky
When thunder and hail threaten your life
Don't fear, don't cry, the Father still keeps an eye.
Amongst the pain 'n confusion His hand will guide
Remember after the storm the sun will again shine

I love you and I will till I take my last breath

With much love xoxo

Your ever-loving yiayia

17 August 2018

To The Groom

Always treat her kindly and gently during day time
and I am sure she will treat you lovingly night time
You may not believe me but you can try it if you like
You will find, it always works like magic, every time.

Don't wait to tell her you love her, close to bed time
She won't believe you, will mock you, won't say why
I have been there; I know she will think it's a big lie
I'm telling you son, this is not love, it is lust in her eye.

She scrubs, washes, shops, cooks and cares for kids
Day after day, for months, years and endless weeks
She does it out of love, there's no wages for her in this
Acknowledge it now and then with a small gift 'n a kiss.

Esther

Irene, my colleague and I were going to Bendigo for a training day, by car. We talked. She expressed my sentiments and experience, and that of countless other women on this planet. This poem was born out of deep empathy for her and all the women with the same experience and is dedicated to them all. It is also a warning to all men, not to take a woman's hard work for granted. I wrote half of it during the training session, and finished it later at home

18 July 2020

Transgender

I look at myself in the mirror wondering if it's really me?
Am I the one I am looking at, or is there another me?

I see a pretty girl in the mirror but that's not the real me.
There is a handsome boy within me, and I know he is me.

Am I one person with two psyches, or two with one psyche?
Mum, dad, I don't know, but please, let me be the real me.

Let me look in the mirror and see the person I was meant to be.
Let me connect with that one, not the wrong body I'm locked in.

Let me find peace of mind, let me be the one I was meant to be.
My appearance will change but my love for you the same will be

Mother nature is wonderful but awry sometimes she goes too.
She creates identical twins and sometimes, conjoint ones too.

Creates a male or female body but locks the wrong psyche in it
Please love the person I really am, it's not my fault why blame me.

Esther

I was watching the evening news when a reported came on the screen who looked female but had a male voice. I thought of the many transgender people I came across, who are intelligent and gifted, but who have been discriminated against, illtreated and laughed at through no fault of their own. I have some understanding of the issues they are facing. Again, I became sad and angry. I put pen to paper and wrote this poem which I dedicate it to all the transgender people in the world and ask the rest to understand that nothing in this world is perfect, including nature, she too gets confused at times

29/11/13

Tribute To Joyce Costa

She was buried on 2/12/13

Today a little light on this earth went out,
She lived her life as best as she knew how,
She is now with God hidden in His heart,
We will remember her with fondness and love.

In our hearts, her spot will always empty remain,
Till on that glorious day when we'll meet her again,
And the Lord, 'well done faithful servant' will say,
And on a new Earth with God forever we will reign.

Dear Joyce, rest in peace, the troubles of this
Earth will never touch you again.
You will always be remembered fondly.

I have known Joyce just on 25 years now; we shared joys, sorrows and pain, but we also shared the pride and joy at the birth of our beautiful granddaughter Jemima.

Feb 26 2018

Tribute To Matthew

His life was suddenly, unexpectantly cut short
For us his handsome face will never grow old
Time will never diminish our love for him at all.

In our memories his name is etched in pure gold
The pain of his loss in our hearts we will always hold
We will never ever forget him in this sad, old world.

I wrote this poem having heard this morning's news that the police killed a young man who they couldn't control. 'They cut his life short' I thought. I remembered Matthew and got upset again. Still in bed I wrote this poem for him and for all the people who died young.

Esther

26 Dec 2018
Ninh Binh,
Vietnam

Understand

Lord I'm confused, my mind is boggled by the things that are said
By those who think they know everything but don't understand
That a Buddha is an Enlighted person and Christ they represent

In every country, people and generation, a Buddha You've sent
From the beginning of time and always, Your love to represent
You are One, with many names, this we must clearly understand.

Lord I strive in my mind and soul, divine things to understand
You are infinite, I'm finite, the infinite, I cannot comprehend
Humbly I ask, cleanse me and with Your Spirit within me dwell.

I long to know, like Jesus I want to become, but I don't know how.
I will not be perfect in this life, hard as I might try, this for I sure know
Please give me humility to say that everything in this life I don't know.

But when I will be changed, in a moment,
in a twinkling of an eye,
At the sound of the last trumpet, like Him
I will be, and to You I'll fly
The limitless universe for ever with Him I
will explore as it goes by.

My eyes will see wonderful things I have
not seen before,
My ears will hear the sweetest sounds I
haven't heard before
We will all be re-united to live on a peaceful
earth for evermore.

I wrote this poem while sitting in an ornate Buddhist temple in Viet Nam, waiting for Miranda and Jemima, (daughter and granddaughter) to return from visiting a sight which was too far, too steep and I was too tired to go. Our egotism and fanaticism in the correctness of our beliefs becomes stark and disconcerting as I grow older. Truth is immense, we only know what has been revealed to us and even then, we interpret it according to our spiritual level, experience and culture, why dismiss everybody else's experience and beliefs, they are just different to ours not necessarily wrong.

Esther

25/8/15
Bermondsey
London

Victoria

Sharp as a razor, quick as a flash
Hot headed as fire, cool as a splash
Loud as a thunder, quiet as a breeze.
When you're with her you are at ease.

She is always happy and jolly galore
Her contagious laughter shakes the floor.
But beware! She erupts like a volcano,
Just make sure, you don't tread on her toe.

The poor little thing couldn't help herself
She is a mixture of all sorts, truly she is.
A father as gentle and calm, as a calm sea
A mother as turbulent as a gale can be.

Her two grandmothers are not far behind
They start a bushfire before you count to five
They get all fired up and hot under the collar
When they talk religion and things on high.

With heredity as varied and colourful as this
She couldn't be anything other than she is.
Smart and quick-witted Victoria always is

My beautiful granddaughter, much loved she is.

I love her and always will, just as she is

Have a wonderful birthday
With much love, xoxoxo

Your-ever loving Yiayia

2/8/13

We Failed You

Little Berny came to this world not so long ago,
She was wanted so much and was treasured so.
Cute as a button and proudly to all she was shown
Mum bubbled with joy; dad's pride was under control.

She was tenderly cared for by her mum and her dad
Her milestones carefully watched and written on a pad.
She is now sitting up and has teeth too, mummy said
She has beautiful blue eyes but has no hair as yet.

Lovingly she was cared for and when she would fall
'Darling, I will kiss it better' sweetly she would be told.
She looked so pretty with a ribbon and her pink dress on
She was the pride and joy of her family and their friends.

Fatigue took over, sleepless nights took their toll
That gorgeous little girl created work for them all
Mum's work was constant; dad couldn't go out at all
Tired and frustrated, they thought it was all her fault.

Dad is too big to be belted; I wouldn't dare do so
I'm so tired and angry, I don't know what to do.
Little Berny was hungry, she grizzled as they do
A belting from her mum, undeservedly copped so.

She couldn't see and could not understand why
She would hide in her room and silently she'd cry
She did no wrong, just in the way she was that time
Crying all the way to school, her bike she would ride.

A vicious circle sat in her family 'it's her fault' they said.
'She's so sullen, so angry; this teenager is as bad as hell'
A lesson we must teach her, let's do it now, let's do it well.'
That she was abused in more ways than one was easy to tell.

As parents, we all try very hard the right thing to do
But we mess up their brains with what we fail to do.
We have no skills, don't know how this tough job to do
Our children are left alone to work out which way to go.

Our parents failed us; their parents did the same too.
They educated us in geography well, in history too.
We learned the intricacies of science 'n physics galore
But how to treat a precious child we were never told.

Our children are angry; they blame us and rightly so.
We blame our parents and they blamed theirs too.
But our schools? They say 'such a good job we do'
Geography is important, teach us good parents to be too.

Having said all that, one more thing I want to say
Teach us from our earliest days what to do and say
Berny, forget what has been done, forward keep going on
And let's pray fervently as He did two thousand years ago,

'Father forgive them all, they didn't know what they should do'.

Esther

I wrote this poem, wishing I knew a better way to bring up my children. Unfortunately, we only get one chance at child rearing. We bring up our children slightly better than we have been brought up ourselves. As parents, we all have regrets which we will take to our graves where they will rest with us. I am glad my children are magnanimous enough to forgive me, for I cannot forgive myself.

25 June 2019

We Let You Go

Dear sister, we are here to bid you good bye,
To celebrate the things, you have loved in life,
To let you go, let your spirit in the clouds fly.

Free as the air, to see beautiful, green fields
To be carried away by the cool, gentle breeze
Over deep oceans, calm lakes, and tall trees.

Your spirit will hover here and the place of your birth
Fly away, you are free from the pains of this earth.
You are in a better place now; you are free as a bird.

We loved you, come to us in our dreams now 'n then
The empty space that you have left in our hearts to fill
Till that wonderful day when we will meet once again.

Your loving sister

Esther

Today, Sunday July 30 we scattered Eleni's ashes on the nature strip at her place on 70 Dall's Road, Whittlesea, where she had planted trees and a lot of yellow jonquils and daffodils. If there is such a thing as our sprits living on and wandering the face of the earth, I know her spirit will be hovering between this place and Rodonia the place of her birth, whereas mine will be all over the face of the earth, but will avoid the whole of Greece.

Monday, 30 March 2020

What Are You?

1. What are you Lord? I don't understand, and I don't know
The more I read and learn about You, the less I seem to follow
The closer I come to You the more insignificant I seem to grow.

2. My importance fades the difference is stark, I'm less than dust.
Please come in, live within me, enlighten me, disperse the dark
Cleanse me, purify me and with Your Holy Spirit fill my soul fast.

3. Lord, I know You are eternal, You are, were, and always will be.
Are you a being? I'm wondering if You too have a form like me?
Are You the wind? maybe not, but are You the power behind it?

4. Are You the light Lord? maybe not, but You filled the world with it.
Are You the fire Lord? no, "Moses take your sandals off, for I am in it"
Are you the blazing furnace Lord? No, but I know you are with me in it

5. Are you the Universe Lord? no, but You are the great power within it
You created the universe by Your word, but how? I don't understand it.
Are you the Energy in it? I am trying hard but I cannot comprehend it.

6. Are you the Spirit which pervades the Universe and fills my soul with it?
Are you the great energy that connects us all together? please reveal it
I know You are. I ask for patience 'n faith till the great mystery is revealed.

7. Jesus said a long time ago, "I will come and live and sup with you"
"As I am in the Father and He in Me, I will also live and be with you"
I accept it, but if this is so, what does that make me, I want to know.

8. Does this make my soul divine, holy and eternal just like You?
Does it make me a demigod, a god powerful and sinless like You?
"No" it doesn't", it just connects us together, we are all one in You.

9. I want to be just like Jesus, caring loving humble and forgiving.
Cleanse me, with Your Spirit fill me, this will make my soul living.
When I see You face to face, I will be pure, with You, I'll be living.

10. For now, one thing I know, that by Your grace, before You I stand,
Please hold me up by Your grace, on my own I know I cannot stand.
Alone I am powerless, I try hard, I stumble, I fall, myself I can't defend

Esther

I couldn't sleep last night again. Read for hours "The Celestine Prophecies" by J. Redfield He says among other things. (I am paraphrasing) something like 'The universe is connected by energy which influences us and we, by concentrating, in turn influence it to behave in a way we expect it to behave' That got me thinking all night. Is that energy that fills the universe God? Do we influence the universe/God, by our prayers which is a kind of concentrating, and which is the only way to connect and commune with God? The bible indicates that God does change His plans/mind, as He did when intending to destroy the wicked city of Nineveh, but because they repented God spared the city, (changed plans). Also, Jesus said, 'ask and it shall be given you' If we concentrate and expect, we influence the Energy/God. And He honours our expectations. It makes sense to me. The words are different but the parallel is uncanny.

22/10/15

Zdenka

You left him unwillingly with pain in you heart
You didn't want to, but you had no choice in that
You trusted your son in my care and that was that.

I promised you faithfully to do the best that I can
Take him lovingly and gently lead him by the hand
To guide and encourage him 'n tell him that he can.

He grew up to be wise in every way imaginable
He's loving 'n caring he has achieved the incredible
If you could see him now, you'd say 'how wonderful'.

I sat by your grave the other day and told you all this
I wept with joy 'n sorrow, you didn't live to see all this
But one day he will sit between us and I'm sure he'll say:

'I had two mothers, one on this earth and one up high'.

I visited Zdenka's grave on my way back from Eleni's. I sat on her grave and thought of her. She lived her short life in joy and sorrow just as all of us on this earth, but with a bit more pain than most. She lost her first sone aged 11 to drowning. She didn't live to see her second son grow up and be the successful person he has become. I went home and wrote this poem for her.

Esther

www.ingramcontent.com/pod-product-compliance
Lightning Source LLC
Chambersburg PA
CBHW072008110526
44592CB00012B/1238